Generosity (Generous City, I like the play on words), is a common English word that means so many varied things to different people. Victor, in this book, has brought very refreshing and inspiring insights to the word. Drawing copiously from the Scriptures, he challenges us to reflect deeply on true stewardship, and the place of money in our lives.

'Generosity is reaching out with what you have received.' 'When money decides your priorities, you are serving money.' 'Whatever you treasure, holds your heart captive.' 'Your generosity is a key part of God's plan to draw others to Him. A generous man or woman lives a life that points others to a generous Father--one they will come to know for themselves.' These and so may more are thought-provoking statements that will enable you to have a clearer perspective of the purpose of the blessings of God in your life. This is so important for the believer especially in these days when 'me, myself, and I' has become the order of the day. I wholeheartedly recommend this book for reading and meditation, not just because the author is my son, but because it is the truth set forth for all. You surely will be blessed reading it.

- DR. JUDE EHIEMERE, *Medical Director, Living Word Mission Hospital, Nigeria and Vice President, Living Word Ministries, Nigeria*

It wasn't until I heard the stewardess say we had to put away our belongings to commence landing procedure, that I realized that I had not stopped reading this book! This piece of art, masterfully crafted under the guidance of Holy Spirit through my brother and friend Victor Ehiemere, took me to a new place on how I will teach generosity for the rest of my life.

In an age where 'generous' is used to avoid saying 'give' or 'money', Victor goes for your throat and addresses the real meaning of generosity from God's intention. To know the substance of this writer is to know that he did not gimmick you in this book, but that he studied, researched and proof texted his argument in the affirmative to support the lifestyle of the generous.

This book is going to perform a heart revolution, and set your spirit free to be generous in every area of your life.

- DERRICK A. GOLDEN, *Senior Pastor, Amazing Church, McKinney, Texas*

Pastor Victor's ability to connect the truth of what The Bible says about generosity to the realities of real life helps us navigate the subject matter through the lens of God with a clarity that refreshes the muddied waters of stewardship. If you are looking for a book that will challenge you to look outside yourself to the needs around you, this book is for you. With grace and truth, Generous City gives us a fresh view on generosity!

- JIM WILKES, Lead Pastor, Journey Community Church, Ohio

What a book! Victor has got me hungry with such a desire to find needs to meet; not just financially, but far beyond. I won't look at the word 'generosity' the same way anymore.

Generosity City is a captivating book which provokes inward assessment of what it means to be generous. Victor has given us permission to see generosity in a new light as it pertains to God, people, and self. If you venture to read this book, you set yourself up to be challenged to a new way of thinking.

- MARCUS ENGLAND, Lead Pastor, The Mix, Baltimore, Maryland

God commissioned Victor to write this life-changing book about generosity! Once this revelation is inside of you, you will not be the same. You'll look at yourself, your world and others completely different. Victor challenges you to think about generosity from God's perspective and in its purest form. When you read this book, you'll be inspired to live a life of giving the way you were created to live!

- BRANDON BARBER, Lead Pastor, Elevate Church, Houston, Texas

Dr. Victor Ehiemere's enthusiasm and energy to engage this important conversation is contagious. This book is the perfect "go-to resource ", easy read for the individual, families, organizations to perpetuate impact and legacy in the current generation and beyond. It takes you from the mere act of generosity to the very life and source of generosity guaranteeing its sustenance and purity. This is a must read and a masterpiece. It's more than information. It's so much life. I am pleased to have the opportunity to participate in what I believe will be a widely read manuscript.

- Dr. PHIL RANSOM BELLO, Lead Pastor, The StandPoint Church, Abuja, Nigeria

GENEROUS CITY is a must-read. Victor takes us on an intentional journey of understanding the all-important subject of giving. His thoughts are compelling, his words are convincing and his writings are captivating. Beware! This book is

addictive and has the potential to positively change your life.
   - RHEMA EHIEMERE, *Visionary Architect, Global Relevance Enterprises*

This book is an eloquent, practical and honest account of God's attributes, heart and love towards his people. Finding your identity in Christ will not only be clear after reading this book but your purpose will also be defined. Definitely a destiny changer and inspiration to say the least.
   - UDEME UMANA, *Director of Living Real Foundation*

The timing of this book could not be any better! Generous City is the blueprint for today's church tore establish the foundations of grace, sacrifice, and giving. Victor Ehiemere brings clarity and passion to a mission that started with Christ. I believe every pastor, leader and Christian needs to read this book.
   - STEVE HARRIS, *Executive Pastor, i5 CHURCH, Maryland, USA*

Compelling. Convicting. Convincing. To challenge everything we know with the boldness of a lion and bring us to a place of authentic stewardship, teaching us our real "why." Pastor Victor Ehiemere has taken something complex and often overlooked, and simplified it so that if we miss it, we only have ourselves to blame. This book is more than a call to do something different; it is a declaration to BE someone different!
   - KASHONNA HOLLAND, *President/CEO, Simply Kashonna*

Generous City is a must read! The pages overflow the goodness and grace of Almighty God. What our cities need is a group of people ready to live dangerously by living generously. Our world desperately needs to see Christ's love through the gentleness of the generosity of His people. I have discovered that true generosity can do surprising things in your life as well. As I began to live a life of generosity, God healed and restored me.

Generosity is the very heart of God. If you want to draw closer to who He is, I challenge you to read this book and challenge yourself to be the most generous version of yourself that you can be! May the world know us by our generosity!
   - CHARITY TRAHAN, *Outreach Director, i5 CHURCH, Maryland, USA*

GENEROUS CITY

11 CONVERSATIONS THAT WILL UNLOCK THE TRUTH AND POWER OF LIVING BEYOND YOURSELF

VICTOR EHIEMERE

© 2016 Victor Ehiemere

All rights reserved. No part of this book maybe reproduced in any form or by any means—electronic, mechanical, photocopy, recording, or any other information storage and retrieval systems—except for brief quotations in printed reviews without the prior written permission of the publishing.

Unless otherwise indicated, all Scripture quotations, marked KJV, are taken from the **KING JAMES VERSION**, Authorized King James Version.

Other Scripture quotations are marked and taken from the following sources:

AMP- Scripture quotations taken from the Amplified Bible, Copyright © 1954, 1958, 1962, 1964, 1965, 1987 by The Lockman Foundation Used by permission. (www.Lockman.org)

CEV - Scripture quotations taken from the Contemporary English Version® Copyright © 1995 American Bible Society. All rights reserved.

GNT – Scripture quotations taken from the Good News Translation® (Today's English Version, Second Edition) Copyright © 1992 American Bible Society. All rights reserved.

GW- Scripture is taken from GOD'S WORD®, © 1995 God's Word to the Nations. Used by permission of Baker Publishing Group.

MSG- Scripture taken from *The Message*. Copyright ©1993, 1994, 1995, 1996, 2000, 2001, 2002. Used by permission of NavPress Publishing Group.

NASB - Scripture taken from the NEW AMERICAN STANDARD BIBLE®, Copyright © 1960,1962,1963,1968,1971,1972,1973,1975,1977,1995 by The Lockman Foundation. Used by permission.

NIV – Scripture quotations taken from THE HOLY BIBLE, NEW INTERNATIONAL VERSION®, NIV® Copyright © 1973, 1978, 1984, 2011 by Biblica, Inc.® Used by permission. All rights reserved worldwide.

NKJV- Scripture taken from the New King James Version. Copyright © 1982 by Thomas Nelson, Inc. Used by permission. All rights reserved.

NLT- Scripture quotations are taken from the Holy Bible, New Living Translation, copyright 1996, 2004. Used by permission of Tyndale House Publishers, Inc., Wheaton, Illinois 60189. All rights reserved.

NLV – Scripture quotations are taken from the New Life Version © Christian Literature International

NRSV – Scripture quotations are taken from the New Revised Standard Version Bible, copyright © 1989 the Division of Christian Education of the National Council of the Churches of Christ in the United States of America. Used by permission. All rights reserved.

PHILLIPS - Scripture quotations are taken from The New Testament in Modern English by J.B Phillips copyright © 1960, 1972 J. B. Phillips. Administered by The Archbishops' Council of the Church of England. Used by Permission.

TLB - Scripture quotations are taken from the Holy Bible, Living Bible, copyright © 1971. Used by permission of Tyndale House Publishers, Inc., Wheaton, Illinois 60189. All rights reserved.

Printed in the United States of America.

ISBN-13: 978-1-5334-3617-7

To Miss Faye Johnson, whose heart for others has been an unabating inspiration to me. In just a few years, I have witnessed what it truly means to live beyond yourself. I am awestruck that even in your fight you make it a duty to constantly help people in their own fight. What a heart!

This is for you, ma'am!

contents

Foreword by Jimmy Rollins i
Foreword by Faye Johnson vii
Introduction ix

Section One: Generosity and God
Chapter 1: God Is Generous 3
Chapter 2: The Great Domino Effect 13
Chapter 3: Generosity Is Spiritual 31
Chapter 4: Jesus And Money 47

Section Two: Generosity and Others
Chapter 5: We are Custodians, Not Owner 63
Chapter 6: The Molds of Custodians 73
Chapter 7: The Profile of A Custodian 91

Section Three: Generosity and Me
Chapter 8: The Blessing of Generosity 101
Chapter 9: The Obedience of Generosity 117
Chapter 10: Lies About Generosity 135
Chapter 11: Generosity As A Memorial 151

Conclusion: The Charge To Generosity 161

Acknowledgments: 167

foreword by Jimmy Rollins

Although I am excited about the contents of this book and how it will change your life, I'm more excited for you to experience the life message and the anointing of the man who penned it. From the moment I met Victor, I have witnessed not just acts of generosity and sacrifice, but a selfless confident heart of a man who lives a message that the world needs. So before we jump into principles that will change your perspective and challenge your lifestyle, let me introduce you to the person who challenged my way of thinking, which changed my way of living.

It was a Sunday morning in 2011. My role that morning as a staff pastor was to transition the service from a worship moment to the announcements and then prepare the congregation for the offering and tithes. As I stood up that day and began to do what had become a monotonous weekly ritual, I had no idea that God had planted a couple who would become a part of launching what we now call i5 CHURCH—a new life-giving church that would wake a visionary who was dying on the vine of complacency and tradition.

That Sunday, in attendance was a young couple full of expectation and vision, but also in evaluation mode. Navigating through a mental church checklist, looking to see if this was the place they would call their church home. Neither of us knew that God had crafted a much greater plan. Over the course of a few weeks, I remember thinking to myself, "Why are they here? What do they want? And where does this guy get his suits made?" Sporting a blue three-piece suit, a fat knot pink tie with a matching pocket square; this dude was dressed for success.

After a few months of regular church attendance, Victor approached me one Sunday for a formal introduction. After we shook hands and exchanged greetings, he gave me a self-published book. He encouraged me to add it to my reading list. He had no idea that I—not only had no interest in reading his book—directly after our introduction, walked back into the office and gave my gift to another pastor on staff instructing him to "Check this guy out!"

Due to my trust issues and the relational wounds of many years in ministry, the vetting process of the man in the three-piece suit was going to be at arm's length. Although I wanted no part of what I thought he was selling, his genuine, selfless, and generous heart spoke loudly. God would not let me ignore nor avoid him.

Following an invitation to his home and the most incredible authentic Nigerian all-you-can-eat spread, God began to fast-forward Victor and Amby's relationship with Irene, and I. Victor began offering his gifts as a graphic artist for the church. That generous act morphed into him helping me grow my leadership influence by taking my sermons and turning them into blogs. It was through writing those blogs and traveling with me on ministry trips that an acquaintance became a friend. A friend quickly became a brother, and as a brother, Victor would eventually become a vital part of God's vision for i5 CHURCH.

The guy, whose book I had discarded like the daily newspaper, was becoming a part of the story God was writing called i5 CHURCH. I remember Victor telling me that somehow he had found out that I gave his gift to me away, and this almost caused him to leave the church. Surely giving his book away was not an act of generosity; it was an act of a guy who trusted no one and was in desperate need of being sharpened by the iron of a brother. Every time I was around Victor and Amblessed, I left challenged in my thoughts and full in my stomach--Amblessed always had a good meal readily available.

There was something different about how they lived. It seemed to me that they had developed a culture in their family of honoring others, living selflessly and believing God for the impossible. I had only seen this in my parent's generation. God was using them to grow something in me that would eventually grow into the values of our new life-giving church. *Living beyond yourself* and *loving beyond your preferences* had become honed and solidified in the fabric of my heart through countless conversations, long study and sermon development sessions, and one moment in our relationship that still makes me a little uncomfortable.

I was in the office one day when Victor and Amby approached me with the confidence of a word from God coupled with a humility that I can't explain. "Pastor Jimmy, We want to sow into your life!" Victor and Amblessed had always honored Irene and me as their pastors and had never done anything less than going above and beyond concerning serving the vision. I knew these words were different.

With tears in his eyes, Victor handed me what I now know was a huge sacrifice for him and his family. He gave me a card that contained words that humbled me to the core and an offering that was more than sacrificial. Victor began to verbalize how they honored us and wanted to sow into Irene and me as an act of obedience and blessing. In a very awkward moment, He described how God had spoken to him and that through this, God wanted to do something supernaturally in his family. What Victor did not know was that through his obedience, God was doing something in me He ultimately wanted to do through me. It was almost as if I saw a reflection of how I was to live. Victor's hands gave me a gift, but God was doing surgery on my heart through his obedience.

What I had just experienced was not a gift from Victor and Amblessed. It was a grace and anointing to accept this gift from God in my life. Through this exchange, a selfish man became a selfless man—one who lived for himself was compelled to live beyond himself. The pursuit of building a life-giving church became my passion.

Fast forwarding about four years, God has used my relationship with the man who wore a three-pieced suit, and whose wife is the best cook I know, to sharpen my soul and shape the vision of a life-giving church that is reaching thousands, locally and globally.

Today, once again, I am saying, "Check this guy out!" Several years ago as a stranger, I gave his book away in an act of disregard, but now, as a brother, I honor the gift of God in Victor.

As you flip through the pages of this book, I encourage you to do more than read the words on these pages. I challenge you to live out the value of living beyond yourself each and every day of your life! I pray that you will be anointed to live with the grace of generosity!

- Jimmy Rollins
Lead Pastor, i5 CHURCH, Maryland, USA

foreword by Faye Johnson

According to man, I am not supposed to be here. I am here only because of HIS GENEROSITY!

I have always considered myself to be a generous person. As a young child, I would give my last piece of candy to a friend if they wanted it. As a teenager, I gave my boyfriend to my best friend (who betrayed our friendship... lol). I have always tried to put the needs of others before mine. Generous, kind, selfless; that is what I thought of myself until I read GENEROUS CITY by Victor Ehiemere.

I have known Pastor Victor for about three years through my partnership with i5 CHURCH. I have watched him grow in his confidence as a speaker and a leader. He has such deep and abiding love for Jesus Christ, and it is evident to anyone who speaks with him. Victor's quest for understanding the teachings of Jesus is exemplified in GENEROUS CITY. His ability to use modern day examples to illustrate the lessons of being sincerely generous, make it easy to understand.

You will experience that 'AHAH' moment when the light comes on. Sometimes, it may make you smile because you found that you did the right thing (even though you didn't fully understand why you did it or the Domino Effect that may occur). Other times, you may feel sad for the many missed opportunities that you had to be generous.

Read GENEROUS CITY, then re-read it! It will transform your life.

I am a recipient of the Domino Effect of God's Generosity!

- Faye G. Johnson
Associate Broker (retired), ReMax Executive

introduction

This book is not about money. It is not a subtle way to convince you to part with your money. That's not my mission. I am gunning for your heart.

This book unveils a master plan to reach the world. I wrote this book as part of a universal mandate and manual that calls and guides us to partner with God to change the world.

When I settled into studying for the sermon that birthed this book, God burdened me with an undying pursuit of the truth about generosity, and living beyond yourself. It is this truth I seek to pass on to you.

Growing up, it was hard to pin me down to eat. I loved drinking water and juices more than I loved chewing. It was so bad that I earned a nickname, *Swallow and Drink Water*. You had to bribe me with water to get me to eat. Joel, my son, is paying me back for this. He packs his food in his left cheek. He once slept with food in his mouth! I have to threaten to take something away to get him to chew and swallow. My mum took a more traditional route to a solution.

Growing up in a Nigerian home, my heightened sense of superstition made me gullible to my mom's mischief. Whenever I gave her a hard time with eating, she threatened to summon a ghost that helped mothers with children who were troublesome. She told me that if she called out three complete times, the ghost would appear and take me away. I was just four years old—I definitely didn't want to see any ghosts!

Before she could call out a three times, I was gulping my food whole and begging for her to stop calling out. Sounds ridiculous now, but my four-year-old self must have been scared stiff of ghosts. The Nigerian TV show, *Willy Willy*[1], didn't help matters.

I lived with this truth for another six years or so. Now I know better, and I feel foolish for falling for such a cheap trick. I should have let her finish her routine at least once and seen what would have happened. I know now what joy my mom found watching me hurriedly comply in fear. This *truth* that my mom sold to me shaped my life for over half a decade.

I am reminded of a story I heard during one of my medical postings to a rural community in southern Nigeria. During a random conversation, I was privy to a story about a family that lived in the village.

For three generations, men from this family fished on the shallow end of the river. Other fishermen would go out into deeper waters while men from this one family chose to remain in the areas they were used to fishing. Months before my visit, the first ever college student from this family came home from his first semester, armed with questions about what he now considered unusual beliefs and behaviors. One of the first

---

[1] A Nigerian TV Show about a ghost of a man that haunts the people who were involved in his murder.

casualties of his inquisition was his family's traditional fishing habits.

His family had boats like every other family but didn't fish in the same depths of water. For some reason they settled for less than other families did. Upon exhaustive inquiry, he discovered something that blew him—and me—away.

Soon after his forefathers settled in the village, the family lost one of their men to a fishing accident. He fell over the boat and drowned—He was a good swimmer. Nobody could explain what happened. And from that day, no one from this family ventured as deep as the man they lost. They became obsessed with the fear that whatever drowned their brother could drown them too.

Three evenings a week, while other boats ventured into deeper, more populated waters, his family settled for what little number and size of fish they could drag in from the shallow end. Months became years, and years became decades. His father, grandfather, uncles and cousins held onto the same old truths, mindset and habits. It's incredible to imagine the hauls of fish they missed out on because of what they believed. They were blinded and crippled by what they believed was true.

Here are my questions for you: What if what you have believed or believe as true is a lie? What if what you have allowed to shape your life is false? What opportunities have you lost because of the lie you believe is true?

Tudor Bismark puts it this way:

> *"Within every human being there is a brain, within every physical brain there is a mind, within every mind there is an attitude or a belief system, within every belief system there is a shaper or molder, within every shaper or molder there is an agenda."*

Our beliefs shape our lives. Our actions and reactions are an expression of what we have accepted as truths. If you believe you deserve more, you will act accordingly. If you believe you are smart, you'll act like you are. And on the other hand, if you believe you are worthless and deserve second best, you'll bow your head in shame and settle for less. What we let in as truth finds its way to our disposition, decisions and actions.

Here is some real truth for you: the devil cannot mess with God's blessing and promise to you. He is powerless to do so. But here is where the enemy finds his strength: he introduces a lie to you. He mixes the truth with some falsehood and when you believe it, he has you hooked!

John 8:44 says the devil doesn't have an iota of the truth in him. In fact, that verse reveals that when the devil lies, he speaks his native language. Imagine that! That means that nothing the devil says or promises is true. Absolutely nothing! Even when it looks like what he promises is pleasurable, it comes with a deadly sting!

Not only does the devil lie; he is also the father of lies. All lies originate from him. Why would you believe anything he has to say? Why would you believe that you are not victorious? Why would you believe that you are not more than a conqueror? Why would you believe that you are a failure? Why would you believe your kids are good for nothing? Why would you believe your marriage will always be terrible? It's a lie. It's always been a lie. The devil is a liar.

The enemy knows he can't curse you because God has blessed you from the beginning of time. All he can do is sell you a lie that displaces you—placing you under a curse. The devil has been crafty from the very beginning. In Genesis 3, he sold a lie to Eve and Adam, which placed all of humanity under a curse. But the story doesn't end there.

When God wants to deliver you, He introduces the truth. When God wants to heal you, He introduces the truth of the healing power that Jesus' stripes bring (Isaiah 53:5). When God wants to assure you of your victory, He shares the truth that you are more than a conqueror (Romans 8:37). When your peace is in question, He reassures you with the truth in Philippians 4:7. God employs His truth to break us from the curse of the lies of the devil.

When God wanted to break us from the curse the disobedience of Adam and Eve put on us, He introduced Jesus. Jesus is the perfect and complete truth of God.

> "I am the way, the truth, and the life!" Jesus answered. "Without me, no one can go to the Father." (John 14:6, CEV)

Jesus is the truth. He doesn't just speak the truth, He is the truth. When He walks into the room, every truth of God's word walks into the room. He doesn't have to speak to tell the truth; He just has to be! Jesus as the truth, broke chains, healed diseases, and raised dead people when He entered the scene.

When Jesus steps into any circumstance, the lies of the devil lose their grip upon our hearts, minds and souls. That's the power of the truth! And Jesus still has this power today!

It's not enough to just know that Jesus is the truth. We have to accept Him as the truth and know the truth for ourselves. In John 8, it says we need to *know* the truth.

And you will know the truth, and the truth will set you free.
(John 8:32, NLT)

The Greek word here for *know* is *ginōskō*. It speaks of sexual intimacy. We must have an intimate knowledge of the truth—as intimate as a sexual experience—if it is going to set us free. Freedom is a fruit of our intimacy with the truth. Head knowledge cannot set you free. Just reading the Bible will not do the trick. Listening to sermons is great, but it will not set you free. You have to know the truth for yourself. You have to be intimate with the truth of God's word to benefit from the freedom it gives. Only an impregnating experience with the truth of God can produce true and lasting freedom.

When I sat down to, first, prepare to preach this sermon, and then, write this book, I had one predominant thought: this needs to be the truth that sets people free to live the higher life God has called them to.

I believe one of the ways the enemy dilutes the power of a God-given opportunity is to strip it down to mere actions. I think generosity—true generosity—has suffered the fate of true worship. We lift our hands, but we do not surrender. We shed tears, but remain unbroken. We sing about His name, but don't know His face. A quick assay reveals that the gift and power of generosity have been diluted by wrong, selfish, Godless teaching. Generosity should not be relegated to just giving—an activity undertaken either because we have been told to or because we want to pacify or silence that selfish voice that resides in every one of us.

In this book, I talk about the spirit and heart of generosity: one stirred spirit stirring another spirit. It's really not about money. It's not the physical action of giving that defines generosity. It is a heart willing to reach beyond selfishness that motivates this lifestyle. The giving part is just a natural consequence of acknowledging and appreciating the grace and blessing of God in your life.

Generosity is not donating—sorry, giving—millions to the less privileged and quickly lining up for an accurate return on our taxes. True generosity is sharing the favor, love, grace and blessings we have received from God with others, and pointing them to the Source in the process. Sometimes, generosity is sharing your food, and sometimes it is volunteering your time to mentor the next generation. It can also be as simple as giving someone a hug or a cup of water. Whatever form it takes, in its truest form, generosity extends God to the people around you.

> *Now that I've put you there on a hilltop, on a light stand—shine! Keep open house; be generous with your lives. By opening up to others, you'll prompt people to open up with God, this generous Father in heaven. (Matthew 5:16, MSG)*

When you are done with this book, I want you to have

experienced the truth about one of God's most powerful gifts to us. And I know this truth will not only set you free to live in the freedom and abundance it triggers, but set you up as a beacon of God's light to a dark, lost and dying world.

My earnest desire is that, by reading this book, you commit to passing on the truths contained in these pages to other people who will, in turn, pass them to others.

You have heard me teach things that have been confirmed by many reliable witnesses. Now teach these truths to other trustworthy people who will be able to pass them on to others. (2 Timothy 2:2, NLT)

- Victor Ehiemere
@victorehiemere
pastorvictor.com

section one:
Generosity and God

***Feel free to post quotes and pictures using the tags #generouscity and @victorehiemere

chapter 1

GOD IS GENEROUS

"… God is the greatest giver in the universe" (Randy Alcorn) [2]

The Bonobos are beautiful but sadly they are endangered great apes. Amongst other remarkable traits, they are known to give out apples, bananas and other fruits to bonobos who aren't a part of their family group. This generous disposition sees Bonobos from different groups travel together for days, or weeks at a time. Their generosity increases their social influence and network.

Dolphins go over and beyond the Bonobos and extend their generosity to species that are not theirs. There are countless stories of swimmers rescued by these cetaceans. A few kind Dolphins have even guided stranded whales back to sea. Dolphins are generally awesome.

---

[2] via www.ChristianQuotes.info

Growing up, my brothers and I never lived alone with our parents. We always had company. First, it was extended family, then *really extended* family and soon non-relatives moved in.

On the evening of my wedding, unknown to my wife and me, my mother fed hundreds of homeless people with the same food served to our guests. She sent people with food packages and drinks to street corners and makeshift shelters! She gave specific instructions that ensured that the quality of the food was not compromised in any way. I wasn't surprised when I learned of this. This is the same woman who hasn't stopped threatening to open her house as a permanent residence for homeless and mentally challenged people. I have seen her care for terminally ill individuals who were left for dead by their families; she nursed them to life. She has shared her life with people you wouldn't notice or remember you met.

As bad as you are, you know how to give good things to your children. How much more, then, will your Father in heaven give good things to those who ask him! (Matthew 7:11, GNT)

Despite the exemplary nature of these illustrations, they are all still pale in comparison to God's incredible love for us. God is generous to everyone! He is generosity personified.

GOD GIVES HIS BEST

"You're familiar with the old written law, 'Love your friend,' and its unwritten companion, 'Hate your enemy.' I'm challenging that. I'm telling you to love your enemies. Let them bring out the

best in you, not the worst. When someone gives you a hard time, respond with the energies of prayer, <u>for then you are working out of your true selves, your God-created selves.</u> This is what God does. He gives his best—the sun to warm and the rain to nourish—<u>to everyone, regardless</u>: the good and bad, the nice and nasty. If all you do is love the lovable, do you expect a bonus? Anybody can do that. If you simply say hello to those who greet you, do you expect a medal? Any run-of-the-mill sinner does that. (Matthew 5:43-47, MSG)

Love your friends. Hate your enemies. It sounds about right; it sounds logical. But it's definitely not God. Jesus challenges us to love everyone, friend or enemy. *"That is what God does."* This is who God is. He generously loves the sinner and the saint, the good and the bad, the righteous and the wicked. He loves because that is who He is. God is Love. He doesn't hold back because we don't deserve it. He loves because He is love, and love cannot help but love. He lavishes His love on our world—unconditional love.

When I stumbled on these verses, I couldn't help but see God bigger than before. It was easy to understand God loved me when I was good, but it blows my mind to think He still loves me even when I am bad. I can't wrap my head around the fact that He loves my friends and the people I can't stand in the same way. God is not just the best at loving. God is love. He gives His best, all the time. It's effortless to give your best when it is convenient—when you have enough to spare or have a deserving recipient. But would you maintain the same standards for someone who didn't recognize, accept, or even reciprocate your love? God holds one universal standard for the priest, the preacher, the sex offender, and the con man. And He invites everyone to receive His love.

This is how much God loved the world: He gave his Son, his one and only Son. And this is why: so that no one need be destroyed; by believing in him, anyone can have a whole and lasting life. (John 3:16, MSG)

Jesus was God's only beloved Son. But most importantly, Jesus was and still is God's best gift to a perishing world. God demonstrated His love to us by giving us Jesus. And this best gift—Jesus—is readily available to everyone who will receive Him. God set the standard for generosity by sacrificing His best and only.

GOD LOVES US IN OUR WORST

Watching an episode of Grey's Anatomy, I was reminded of my time as a medical doctor. In this episode, Dr. Meredith Grey is caring for a patient who is going in and out of consciousness. After a bout of seizures, her patient attacks her, breaking her jaw, elbow, ribs, and some other bones I cannot recall right now. Both of them—victim and assailant—were found unconscious on the emergency room floor. She wasn't able to hear or speak for weeks. Her kids wouldn't come near her because they were frightened by the wires in her mouth. It was hard to watch her go through it.

After about six weeks of recovery, she discovers that her

attacker couldn't remember what had transpired—*postictal memory loss*. What was she supposed to do? Simply forgive him because he didn't do it intentionally? Please! That was easier said than done. She reserved every right to hold onto her anger. It didn't matter what state her attacker was in; he had no justification to cause her that much pain. Personally, it would have taken a miracle for me to forgive the gravity of that sort of attack. Slap me on the face, and I might forgive you in an hour, depending on who was watching. Break my jaw, elbow, knees and ribs, and rupture my eardrum while you are at it, and forgiveness might never be on the cards.

If Dr. Grey or I were God, the world would be a very different place. Most people would be confined by the sins and mistakes of the worst seasons of their lives. But thank God that He is God because He specializes in giving us His best, especially in our worst state. God forgives sins—small and great—with the same freeing grace! It's left to us to receive this gift of grace (and also our responsibility to ensure that we don't confuse this gift as a license to keep living against God's will).

> *We were weak and could not help ourselves. Then Christ came at the right time and gave His life for all sinners. No one is willing to die for another person, but for a good man someone might be willing to die. But God showed His love to us. While we were still sinners, Christ died for us. (Romans 5:6-8, NLV)*

God didn't and doesn't wait for it to be convenient to love us. He reached down—deep down—into the mess we were in and loved us back to life. When we deserved death, God sent

His Son, Jesus, to die in our stead. When we deserved condemnation to darkness and sorrow, He brought us His light and joy. God doesn't just love us in our worst; He makes us our best from our worst.

There is a remarkable story of a father-son relationship in Luke 15 that is quite exceptional. The son asks for his inheritance while his father is still alive. His father graciously bequeaths his portion to him. The son leaves home, loses his sensibilities and squanders His father's wealth on frivolous living. One day, while feeding pigs with some leftover food he wasn't even allowed to eat, he came to his senses, and decided to return home.

It was evident to this son that he didn't deserve the place of a son anymore. He was willing to settle for being a mere servant in his father's house. He didn't expect a hug or warmth of any sort. He didn't anticipate a smile. This was not supposed to be a sweet reunion. It's not like he was coming home with the returns on investing his inheritance. There was nothing to be proud of. A reluctant nod of the head and a gesture towards the servants' quarters was the best he could have hoped for— no, the best he was *praying* for! The greatest Hollywood producers could not have scripted his father's reaction.

> *So he returned home to his father. <u>And while he was still a long way off</u>, his father saw him coming. Filled with love and compassion, <u>he ran to his son, embraced him, and kissed him</u>. "But his father said to the servants, 'Quick! Bring the finest robe in the house and put it on him. Get a ring for his finger and sandals for his feet. And kill the calf we have been fattening. We*

must celebrate with a feast, for this son of mine was dead and has now returned to life. He was lost, but now he is found.' So the party began. (Luke 15:20, 22-24, NLT)

Other than the sacrifice of Jesus, if there is a better picture of God's generosity, I am yet to see it. The father ran! If he waited for him to get home and gave him a hug, it would still have been an over-the-top reaction. But he ran, hugged and kissed his disgraceful son. The running speaks about anticipation. It is not difficult to imagine that the father might have stood on that porch every day since his son left, praying that he returned. He just didn't pray that his son returned; he prepared for it—he had a calf fattening for this occasion.

The father was ready to forgive before his son began his journey home. On this day, the son's out-of-this-world prayer was answered. The father saw the frail frame in the horizon and recognized it was his son. This frame was skinnier, smelly, unkempt, and dressed in rags, but it was his son. The emerging figure was the worst state the son had ever been in, but it evoked the best feeling and action the father ever had.

To the father, his son deserved the very best, even in his worst state. The best robe in the whole house was placed on him—probably after he had taken a good bath. The best ring and sandals were fitted on his finger and feet respectively. And finally a calf—the especially fattened calf—was killed for the son who had squandered everything he inherited. God is generous like that, especially in our worst of times and states.

GOD ALWAYS GIVES MORE THAN ENOUGH

I think the moment my fatherhood dawned on me was when I walked out of a store with shopping bags filled with clothes and shoes for my son. Okay, it might not be remarkable until you understand that I went in with an original plan to shop for myself. How I stood at that H&M cash register paying for just kids clothing and shoes still baffles me. Some other day, I rushed in to buy a pair of pants for him and came out with three pants and three sweaters—really cool sweaters, I must say! I don't know how it happens!

When I am not unconsciously shopping for that little man who thinks he owns the world and commands us alike (I digress), I am buying more things than he needs. Joel has outgrown shoes and clothes he has not worn a single day in his life. I am not proud of it, but there are boxes of toys he is yet to open, not to talk of play with. Sometimes, I think he is just spoilt.

Joel's godparents, *uncles*, and *aunties* don't help the matter. They take him on *quick* shopping trips, and come back with boxes—I mean actual big boxes—of toys. One time, he came back with two pieces of the same toy. Why?!? I have had to send a godparent home with a box of toys because I had no room to store it—who buys an inflatable slide for a child in the winter? I would have to store it for five months before I used it. Help a brother here! My friend has come home from trips with size 5 and 6 shoes he *couldn't help but buy* for his little man. They all fall for his charm. I don't blame them; I do too! I am grateful he has them in his life.

God is like Joel's godparents. When He gives, He always gives more than enough. The almighty nature of God—*El Shaddai*—is closely tied to His satisfying, nourishing, and supplying nature, just as a mother would her child.

> *<u>And God will generously provide all you need</u>. Then you will always have everything you need and plenty left over… (2 Corinthians 9:8, NLT)*

> *You treat me to a feast, while my enemies watch. You honor me as your guest, and <u>you fill my cup until it overflows</u>. (Psalm 23:5, CEV)*

When God gives, it overflows. God is a more-than-enough God. When God heals, He heals and restores. When God saves, He saves and delivers. When God provides, He provides and protects. God doesn't just fill your cup; He pours till it runs over. Everything you and I could ever need can be found in our more-than-enough, all-sufficient God.

Here is the secret. First, God created all things in Himself, and then He created us. He did this because He wanted us to have all things we need already provided in Him. God is our source, and all we need is in Him. God's all for us is more than we will ever need.

> *God can do anything, you know—far more than you could ever imagine or guess or request in your wildest dreams! (Ephesians 3:20-21, MSG)*

One day, Joel will be able to ask beyond my resources and ability to provide for him. I will always try to do my best for him, but someday my best will not cut it. But with God, that will never be the case. None of us could ever dream, imagine, pray or request more than God can deliver. That's for sure!

GOD IS GENEROUS

God lays down an excellent example of generosity in the way He loves you, me and everyone in the world—born and unborn. God's generosity inspired Him to create a garden for Adam and Eve. That same generosity led Him to sacrifice His one and only Son for our redemption. Our unworthiness or sins do not restrict His generosity. The more unworthy we are, they more willing He is to give for us, we just need to accept it!

> *Every good thing given and every perfect gift is from above; it comes down from the Father of lights (the Creator and Sustainer of the heavens), in whom there is no variation (no rising or setting) or shadow cast by His turning (for He is perfect and never changes). (James 1:17, AMP)*

chapter 2

THE GREAT DOMINO EFFECT

Open your hands, ye Whose hands are full! The world is waiting for you! The whole machinery of the Divine beneficence is clogged by your hard hearts and rigid fingers. Give and spend, and be sure that God will send; for only in giving and spending do you fulfill the object of His sending. (Josiah Gilbert Holland) [3]

President Dwight D. Eisenhower—the 34th President of the United States—coined a term that would govern the US foreign policy for about forty years when he suggested that the fall of the French-colonized Indochina to communists would result in the fall of neighboring territories. Even though his words had little immediate significance—one month later, Dien Bien Phu fell to the communists—the phrase he coined has stood the test of time. That phrase is 'Domino Effect'.

---

[3] Gilbert, J. H. (1895). *Dictionary of burning words of brilliant writers: A cyclopædia of quotations from the literature of all ages.* New York: W.B. Ketcham.

I don't know how to play the game of dominoes, but I know a whole lot about Domino Effect. The Merriam-Webster dictionary defines Domino Effect as *a cumulative effect produced when one event initiates a succession of similar events*. In simpler terms, this phenomenon occurs when one action leads to many other actions back to back to back.

I am convinced that even before President David "Ike" coined the phrase, God already employed this strategy in His operations. God is a master of the Domino Effect. Nothing He does is one off. He works with a process, a chain reaction—a succession of events and relationships—in mind. He created plants that work with carbon dioxide through photosynthesis to produce glucose and oxygen. The oxygen molecules are then inhaled by human beings who exhale air with 100 times more carbon dioxide than they inhaled. So in essence, plants *breathe in* what humans breathe out and vice versa.

Here is what I consider a good example of God's Domino Effect. In Acts 7, we see the account of the first Christian martyr. The story seems to be a singular, extraordinary event until you read the latter part of verse 58.

> *His accusers took off their coats and laid them at the feet of a young man named Saul. (Acts 7:58, NLT)*

In this verse, we meet Saul. In what seemed like an insignificant name-drop, we meet the man who took care of the clothes of the men who stoned Stephen to death. Stephen's death seems like another great Christian event until we realize that his boldness—and willingness to die—in the last verse of chapter 7 introduces us to a world-changer whose name was later changed to Paul.

Now here is my question. Did Stephen's courage to stand for God in the face of death play some part in the activation of soon-to-be Apostle Paul? Was Saul's presence around that death-hole more than just because he was a trusted ally of the Synagogue of the Libertines (Acts 6:9)? I don't think so. It surely sounds like there is more to the plot.

I don't think God was thinking just about Stephen. And He was not just thinking about Apostle Paul who took the gospel far beyond any of the original disciples and wrote half of the New Testament. He was thinking about you and me, and the millions of people who—by God's Domino Effect—have come to know and love Jesus. One man witnessed another man's courageous death and went on to be one of the greatest witnesses of God's grace to the world.

GOD'S CREATION PLAN

In Genesis 1, at creation, God could have just created trees, plants, land and sea animals, and done it all over again every month, year or so. It would have been time-consuming and intensive, but God is almighty, and that would not have been a challenge. But this is what He did:

> *Then God said, "Let the land sprout with vegetation—every sort of <u>seed-bearing plant</u>, and trees that grow <u>seed-bearing fruit</u>.*

> *These seeds will then produce the kinds of plants and trees from which they came." And that is what happened.*
>
> *The land produced vegetation—all sorts of seed-bearing plants, and trees with seed-bearing fruit. <u>Their seeds produced plants and trees of the same kind.</u> And God saw that it was good.*
>
> *Then God said, "Let the waters swarm with fish and other life. <u>Let the skies be filled with birds of every kind</u>." So God created great sea creatures and every living thing that scurries and swarms in the water, and every sort of bird—each producing offspring of the same kind. And God saw that it was good.*
>
> *Then God said, "Let the earth produce every sort of animal, each producing offspring of the same kind—livestock, small animals that scurry along the ground, and wild animals." And that is what happened. God made all sorts of wild animals, livestock, and small animals, each able to produce offspring of the same kind. And God saw that it was good. (Genesis 1:11-12, 20-12, 24-25, NLT)*

Every tree and plant had within it the next generation of trees and plants. Every species of fishes and birds was created with the capacity and capability to produce other fishes and birds. Every land animal—small and large—was also created with the next 200 and more generations in mind. God could have created new birds, fishes, cows and lions every morning, but He chose to give each generation the capacity to produce the next generation. This is another example of God's Domino Effect.

God didn't retire this strategy when man was created.

2: The Great Domino Effect

Adam was created from the dust of the earth (Genesis 2:7) and after some *lonely* hours, days or weeks, God decided to create a companion for Adam. With this decision, God was presented with another opportunity to create without reference to any pre-existing creature. Nevertheless, He stuck with His usual strategy.

> *So the Lord God caused the man to fall into a deep sleep. While the man slept, the Lord <u>God took out one of the man's ribs</u> and closed up the opening. Then the Lord <u>God made a woman from the rib</u>, and he brought her to the man. (Genesis 2:21-22, NLT)*

For as long as the first man was alive, the first woman was locked in him. God took from Adam to make Eve. Just like the seeds for the next generations of trees are locked up in the fruits of the first trees, the first woman existed in the first man.

Guess what happens when a child is to be born. A portion of the man and woman—DNA—is passed to the offspring. God is powerful enough to create 350,000 babies every day to replace the over 150,000 people who die every day. He is all-powerful! But He has chosen to conceal the next generation of humans in this generation of humans. Adam and Eve were the first two tiles in God's master Domino Effect to fill the earth with people. And He made this clear when He blessed them.

> *Then God blessed them and said, "Be fruitful and multiply. Fill the earth…" (Genesis 1:28, NLT)*

And even when God destroyed the earth with a flood (Genesis

7), He had yet another opportunity to start afresh with no references. Instead of creating everything afresh, He preserved a sample of creation as a seed—first tiles—for the coming generations of living things.

Every living thing God created can reproduce. What exists now can produce what will be. God could have created every invention there is and will be, but He gave us brains and inquisitive minds to question, create and produce. We don't just have the capacity to reproduce; we have the power, authority and—I dare say—the responsibility to do so. That is how the Domino Effect works: one tile has the energy and responsibility to knock the next tile down.

OUR PRINCIPAL ASSIGNMENT

Sometimes, reading the Scriptures can seem a tad redundant especially when you are conversant with the text you are reading. But it is in the familiar that God hides mysteries that unlock deeper revelations and higher dimensions of living. My eyes were recently opened to the mysteries of one of those familiar scriptures.

In Genesis 2:7, after God created man, it says He *breathed the breath of life* into Adam's nostrils, and man became a living soul. Sounds mundane. Sounds plain. But in this ordinary text, God buried the very reason we exist.

If God breathed into Adam's nostrils to bring him to life, it means that the first thing Adam did when he became a living being was breath out. Do you get it? The first thing the first human did was give out what God gave to him. We exist to give away what God has given to us. We were not designed to hoard what God gave to us. We are purposed to freely give away what we have freely received.

> *"Generosity could be as contagious as the zombie plague as long as enough people were willing to be carriers."* (Jonathan Maberry) [4]

Hold your breath. Hold it. Hold it. Do you feel your life sneaking away from you? We die slowly when we withhold what God has designed to be shared with the world. When we hold our breath, we suffocate. When we withhold our worship, our spirit—our connection to God—dies. When we restrain our love, our relationships die. God intended that we share our lives. My friend and pastor, Jimmy Rollins, puts it this way, "If you're not giving life, you're not living life."

In our lives—in the sharing of it—lie the lives of other people. The world around us is dying. Hopelessness, despair and despondency are the order of the day. There is more bad news than good on the 7 o'clock news. Our world is in need of a spiritual CPR. We need people who are willing and selfless enough to share their breath—their lives—with others. We need to resuscitate our world with the freeing grace and transformative love of Jesus. That is our principal assignment as ambassadors of God's Kingdom. God uses us to bless the world around us.

---

[4] Maberry, J. (2011). *Dust & decay.* New York: Simon & Schuster BFYR.

BLESSED TO BE A BLESSING

Ever heard the song *Abraham's Blessings Are Mine*? During my research for this book, I realized that I have sung a very interesting—polite way for saying *wrong*—version of the song all my life. No matter what version you grew up singing in Sunday School, one thing was clear: the words have us claiming the blessing of an obedient man called Abraham. And we are right to do so. Here is why:

> *Christ redeemed us from that self-defeating, cursed life by absorbing it completely into himself. Do you remember the Scripture that says, "Cursed is everyone who hangs on a tree"? That is what happened when Jesus was nailed to the cross: He became a curse, and at the same time dissolved the curse. And now, because of that, the air is cleared and we can see that <u>Abraham's blessing is present and available for non-Jews, too</u>. We are all able to receive God's life, his Spirit, in and with us by believing—just the way Abraham received it. (Galatians 3:13-14, MSG)*

The promises of God to Abraham are available to all of us through the sacrifice of Jesus Christ. His death, burial and resurrection bridged the gap and cleared the way for us. Jesus connected us to the blessings of Abraham. Let's explore Abraham's encounter with God.

In Genesis 12, God calls a 75-year-old Abram (aka Abraham) from his native land and people to a land and life unknown. In the very many uncertainties that accompanied this call lay some definite assurances.

2: The Great Domino Effect

And I will make you a great nation, And I will bless you, And make your name great; And so you shall be a blessing; And I will bless those who bless you, And the one who curses you I will curse. And in you all the families of the earth will be blessed. (Genesis 12:2-3, NASB)

God blessed Abraham for his obedience. God made Abraham's name great—we are still talking about him today, and for good reason. God rewarded his extreme obedience with greatness, prosperity, and legacy. Abraham went on to be and be called the Father of Faith. Let's take another look at the blessings God pronounced on the Father of Many Nations:

- *I will make you a great nation*
- *I will bless you*
- *I will make your name great*
- *You will be a blessing*
- *I will bless those who bless you and curse those who curse you*
- *In you, all the nations of the earth will be blessed*

In this declaration, we have six statements: 4 benefits and 2 responsibilities. God had His part, and Abraham had his. Sometimes, we get so excited about the promise that we loose sight of the responsibility that usually accompanies the former. There is always a premise to the promise. You must be up for the responsibility if you are going to see the promise fulfilled.

God was going to bless Abraham all right, but there was some work to be done on Abraham's part. Take a look at Abraham's duty list:

- *Be a blessing with the blessing you are, and*

- Bless all the nations of the earth

That means the greatness, notoriety and protection were not just for Abraham. It was for all the nations of the earth. God was thinking about all the nations of the earth when He called Abraham. God called a man to be the first tile of the Domino Effect in the nation of faith He was looking to establish. Abraham was not a one-off blessed man. In his blessing lay the blessing of every one from any nation of earth who got in right relationship with God. First, this blessing in Abraham was just for Jews, but Jesus opened this up to everyone who acknowledges and accepts His sacrifice for their sin.

SALT, LIGHT, AND FISHERMEN

Jesus—our bridge to Abraham's blessing—came with a radiating gospel. By radiating, I mean that He took the gospel wherever He went to whomever He met. Even though we have every right to personalize the ministry and mission of Jesus, He came for the billions of people who call earth their home.

Practically, during His stay on earth, Jesus walked about, going from city to city, village to village, healing the sick and spreading the gospel of freedom and more abundant life (Acts 10:38). He didn't stick to one town or one family or His friends. He took the gospel to every place He went. And when He chose His disciples, He was clear that they were mandated to live beyond themselves.

> *Walking along the beach of Lake Galilee, Jesus saw two brothers: Simon (later called Peter) and Andrew. They were fishing, throwing their nets into the lake. It was their regular work. Jesus said to them, "Come with me. I'll make a new kind of fisherman out of you. I'll show you how <u>to catch men and women</u> instead of perch and bass." They didn't ask questions, but simply dropped their nets and followed. (Matthew 4:18-20, MSG)*

The Domino Effect had begun. A rabbi imparted grace to a fisherman, and that fisherman influenced his brother (John 1:41), and so on. One man, Jesus, came with the message of love from God, but now He had 12 men who were willing to reach out to other people with this freeing power. This was the Master plan: reach ordinary men and women who would, in turn, reach other ordinary men and women—one tile knocking down the next tile. Jesus came to kick start the Domino Effect.

Until our walk with God is contagious, we are not manifesting the fullness of the gospel of Jesus Christ. The love that Jesus puts in our hearts is communicable—it should spread to everyone you come in contact with.

In Matthew 5, Jesus calls us the salt of the earth. If there is anything to know about salt, it is that it lives for everything around it. Salt exists to either preserve or enhances the taste of whatever it is mixed with. Everyone who relates with you should feel your salt nature. Extend the preserving grace of Jesus beyond the four walls of your condo or church. Be the conduit through which people taste their purpose in God. Be the salt of the earth. If we abandon this responsibility as salt, we are no longer relevant to God's plan on the earth (Matthew 5:13).

> *Let me tell you why you are here. You're here to be salt-seasoning that brings out the God-flavors of this earth. If you lose your saltiness, how will people taste godliness? You've lost your usefulness and will end up in the garbage. (Matthew 5:13, MSG)*

Jesus also calls us the light of the world.

> *"Here's another way to put it: <u>You're here to be light</u>, bringing out the God-colors in the world. <u>God is not a secret to be kept. We're going public with this</u>, as public as a city on a hill. If I make you light-bearers, you don't think I'm going to hide you under a bucket, do you? <u>I'm putting you on a light stand.</u> Now that I've put you there on a hilltop, on a light stand—<u>shine!</u> Keep open house; <u>be generous with your lives. By opening up to others, you'll prompt people to open up with God, this generous Father in heaven.</u> (Matthew 5:14-16, MSG)*

You are not here to enjoy the light and life of God all to yourself. You are here to be light in the world. Our encounter with God is of little consequence if it is not shared with the people proximal, and even distal, to us. God didn't save you to stow you away in eternity. He saved you and made you a light carrier in your family, at your job, your kid's soccer game and neighborhood. When we receive from God, our first obligation, after we have enjoyed and embraced the experience, is to shine! If a candle or light bulb doesn't illuminate the space around it, it is useless. Nobody wants to be useless, especially to God.

Notice what the light conversation leads to—generosity. The text doesn't say be generous with your money, time or talent. It says *"...be generous with your lives"*! Generosity should not be compartmentalized. It should not be expressed through one aspect of your life and neglected by the rest. Generosity is not what you do one day a week, probably in church or on the weekends. It should not be an occasional act or gift. It is not something we *remember* or are remind to do. It should not just be relegated to a line item on your budget, personal or organizational. Jesus commands us to be generous with our lives—every single day of it.

We must be open with our lives. I am not asking you to let yourself be taken advantage of. I implore you to ask God to use whatever He will to touch the lives of people you encounter. Today it might be your smile, and tomorrow it might be a hug. The day after it might be the small denominations you have in your car or it may be mentoring a lost teen. Our prayer should be that we are open to let God use whatever He chooses to knock the next tile in His Domino Effect. This is how a city is reached—when every light-bearer lights the lamp next to it. Your generosity—your shining—prompts people to open up to God. Your generosity is a key part of God's plan to draw others to Him. A generous man or woman lives a life that points others to our generous Father—one they will come to know for themselves.

HOW GREED CHOKED A MAN

There are a few kinds of people the Bible refers to as fools. Here are some examples:
- *People who say there is no God (Psalm 14:1)*
- *People who slander or damage other people's reputation (Proverbs 10:18)*
- *People who despise their father's instruction (Proverbs 15:5)*
- *People who trust in their own understanding more than in God (Proverbs 28:26)*
- *Lazy or idle people (Ecclesiastes 4:5)*
- *People who talk too much and base their arguments on empty assumptions (Ecclesiastes 10:13-14)*

In Luke 12, while teaching on greed and it's destructive end, Jesus shares a profound story that introduces us to another kind of fool.

Then he told them a story: "A rich man had a fertile farm that produced fine crops. He said to himself, 'What should I do? I don't have room for all my crops.' Then he said, 'I know! I'll tear down my barns and build bigger ones. <u>Then I'll have room enough to store all my wheat and other goods.</u> And I'll sit back and say to myself, "My friend, you have enough stored away for years to come. Now take it easy! Eat, drink, and be merry!"'

"But God said to him, '<u>You fool!</u> You will die this very night. Then who will get everything you worked for?'

"Yes, a person is a fool to store up earthly wealth but not have a rich relationship with God." (Luke 12:16-21, NLT)

When you operate in greed, the number of references to your person in your vocabulary and lifestyle goes way up. In the short story above, the rich fool referred to himself 15 times (first and second person).

This man received in measures he didn't anticipate. He received more than he could hold. Even though his farm was fertile, he obviously didn't anticipate a harvest as massive as what he brought in. And at that moment he was faced with two choices. He chose the worse of them. Instead of thinking of how he could be a blessing to others, He chose to tear down his current barn and build a larger one to store *everything* for himself.

> *If you start thinking to yourselves, "I did all this. And all by myself. I'm rich. It's all mine!"—well, think again. Remember that <u>God, your God, gave you the strength to produce all this wealth</u> so as to confirm the covenant that he promised to your ancestors—as it is today. (Deuteronomy 8:17-18, MSG)*

Isn't it interesting how we can pray for open doors and blessings from God, and when our prayers are answered, we quickly shut our doors and windows? When in need, our prayers turn to begging sessions, we worship harder and longer, lifting our hands and voices in songs of God's goodness. But when we get that raise or new job, we suddenly think we did it all by ourselves. Deuteronomy 8 encourages us to rethink our stances when we are tempted to play God. We must be as humble before God when our needs are met as we were when we were in need.

The rich fool fell hard into the God-complex. His posture suggests that he was deceived by the abundance he received, and lacked the necessary wisdom to handle it. How could he predict the future? How did he know he was going to be alive long enough to enjoy all that he now owned? When we think all we have is ours, we play the role of both the Provider and the *providee*. Greed and self-absorption positions you to lose everything, even the things that are for your enjoyment.

IT'S NOT ALL YOURS!

There is the one who (generously) scatters (abroad), and yet increases all the more; and there is the one who withholds what is justly due, but it results only in want and poverty. <u>The generous man (is a source of blessing and) shall be prosperous and enriched,</u> and he who waters will himself be watered (reaping the generosity he has sown). (Proverbs 11:24-25, AMP)

A portion of everything you receive is to be shared or given away. The receipt must provoke generosity if it is going to unlock the fullness of the manifold blessings of God. Here is the Domino Effect perspective: some energy spent knocking down your tile must be used to knock down the next tile. If you hoard the gifts and grace transferred to you when you were blessed, you halt God's strategy to reach the world. It's that simple.

The rich fool died because he withheld what was not his. He didn't die for holding onto his rightful portion. This man died because he thought more to him meant more for him. He refused to be a conduit, and settled for life as a container and consumer. God gives us more so that we give out more. When there is an increase in your harvest, there should be an equal or more increase in your seed. Greed says, 'Increase your barn.' Generosity says, 'Increase your seed.'

> *And God will generously provide all you need. <u>Then you will always have everything you need and plenty left over to share with others.</u> As the Scriptures say, "They share freely and give generously to the poor. Their good deeds will be remembered forever."*
>
> *For God is the one who provides seed for the farmer and then bread to eat. In the same way, <u>he will provide and increase your resources and then produce a great harvest of generosity in you.</u>*
>
> *Yes, you will be enriched in every way so that you can always be generous. And when we take your gifts to those who need them, they will thank God. (2 Corinthians 9:8-11, NLT)*

God's generosity to us is a seed that produces a great harvest of generosity in our hearts. And what we give out is a seed that grows into lives dedicated and grateful to Jesus. That's God's divine plan—His Domino Effect. God doesn't want you to stop at prosperity—that's good and okay, but that's not all. God wants you to move on to generosity. Prosperity doesn't multiply and create life change until it is transformed to generosity.

Everything God does or gives is designed to reach far beyond one person, tribe or nation. Our faith—this light we carry—is only as potent as how often it is transferred. Living generously postures us to be conduits of God's miraculous grace to a world in dire need. Generosity sends out a portion of the God in you to touch the lives of the people around you.

> *... be generous with your lives. By opening up to others, you'll prompt people to open up with God, this generous Father in heaven. (Matthew 5:16, MSG)*

> *What do you think God gave you more wealth than is requisite to satisfy your rational wants for, when you look around and see how many are in absolute need of that which you do not need? Can you not take the hint?* [5]

---

[5] Gilbert, J. H. (1895). *Dictionary of burning words of brilliant writers: A cyclopædia of quotations from the literature of all ages.* New York: W.B. Ketcham.

chapter 3

GENEROSITY IS SPIRITUAL

Wealth tends to materialize the soul. Every contribution to spiritual objects counteracts the tendency. It is another step up the ladder, whose foot is deep down in materialism, but whose top reaches to the holy heavens of spirit and love. (Jean de La Bruyère) [6]

I am convinced that only people who have experienced true grace extend grace to others. If you believe you don't need redemption, you make it a duty to make sure people get the full wrath of the law. Grace and mercy trigger grace and mercy. A holier-than-thou heart cannot generate the grace others might need.

A while ago one of my friends brought a story to my

---

[6] Gilbert, J. H. (1895). *Dictionary of burning words of brilliant writers: A cyclopædia of quotations from the literature of all ages.* New York: W.B. Ketcham.

attention. A pastor had fallen. His congregation had forsaken him, and the media wouldn't let the story go. My friend went on and on, expressing his frustration with Christian leaders abusing their platforms indiscriminately. He was convinced this pastor deserved all that was happening and coming to him. The more he spoke, the quieter I became. It must have been 15 minutes, and I hadn't said a word. I hadn't nodded or provided the proverbial 'Hmmm'. I was lost in thought.

What right did I have to throw a stone in judgement against this pastor? Was I so holy that I could stand in righteous indignation against him? I was reminded of the story of the woman caught in adultery in John 8. The Pharisees tested Jesus with a real-life scenario. They presented a woman caught in adultery and demanded His opinion on the lawful consequence of being stoned to death. (Ever wondered about the man she was caught with?)

In a moment of pure wisdom, Jesus asks anyone holy enough—without sin—to throw the first stone. If the crowd could produce one sinless man or woman, they could stone her to death. Your guess is as good as mine. Some shameful secret misdeeds must have flashed through every mind in attendance. And one by one, her accusers began making their way home. A crowd that was frothing at the mouth with judgement resorted to grace when they realized how much grace they needed.

I am not attempting to excuse any sinful actions. I am all for justice and consequence. That's not my point. I am not just quick to jump to judgement because I know where I am coming from and what I am capable of. I am convinced that, if left to my vices, I would ruin every good thing God has and will do in my life. It is the grace I experience from God that compels me to show grace. It is the fact that I know I don't deserve any platform I have that humbles me. It rips the wig off my head and snatches the gavel from my hand. It draws me away from the magistrate's bench. It doesn't make me condone indiscretion but drives me to my knees in prayer. I pray that God covers the sinner just as He has to cover me each day.

... we are just as capable of messing it up as they were. Don't be so naive and self-confident. You're not exempt. You could fall flat on your face as easily as anyone else. Forget about self-confidence; it's useless. Cultivate God-confidence. (1 Corinthians 10:11-12, MSG)

STIRRED SPIRITS STIR OTHER SPIRITS

You cannot give from an empty place. Only a heart stirred by God can reach out to others. That is a governing principle of generosity. Generosity is born when God touches our hearts and spirits. It doesn't start with a paycheck. Generosity begins with a stirred spirit. It is in this context that we must understand that generosity is, first of all, spiritual.

Generosity is not a physical exercise. It manifests in the physical what already exists in the spiritual. When your spirit is touched and stirred, it naturally compels you to reach out, touch and stir another spirit—sharing what you have received.

Generosity is sharing, with another spirit, what your spirit has been blessed with. That is why we cannot confine generosity to the limits of just money. Money-talk pervades any generosity conversation because that is the currency we are most conversant with. But that's not all the currency there is.

Faith is a currency. By faith, we access spiritual dimensions we could never experience otherwise. Mercy is a currency. According to Matthew 5:7, you *obtain* mercy when you are merciful. Forgiveness is a currency. When we forgive, we walk in God's forgiveness (Matthew 6:9-12, 14-15, Mark 11:25). Humility is a currency. It unlocks God's hand to exalt you (Matthew 23:12). These are a few of the spiritual currencies that we trade in. Generosity is myopic when it is relegated to what we do with our money. If our hearts are trading in the right currencies, the money currency gets sorted out by natural consequence. Even though these spiritual currencies are important, there is still no denying that the way we handle our money is a good representation of the state and passion of our hearts (Luke 12:34).

THE HOLY SPIRIT GETS MAD

The first account we have of the Holy Spirit getting upset is found in Acts 5. And it was about generosity. In the text, Ananias and his wife Sapphira did what everyone around them was doing, but their story didn't end like anyone else'.

The early church was growing by leaps and bounds, and one of the defining characteristics of their community was that they shared everything they had in common. No one lacked for anything. People sold their lands and other possessions and submitted the proceeds to the apostles who made it available to all according to the needs.

> *All the believers were united in heart and mind. <u>And they felt that what they owned was not their own, so they shared everything they had.</u> The apostles testified powerfully to the resurrection of the Lord Jesus, and God's great blessing was upon them all. <u>There were no needy people among them</u>, because those who owned land or houses would sell them and bring the money to the apostles to give to those in need. (Acts 4:32-35, NLT)*

If everyone was doing it, why did Ananias and Sapphira end up unlike everyone else? This couple died. After the sale of their land, they decided to misrepresent their gift to the apostles. They claimed what they were giving was all they made. Their actions show that they thought generosity was just a physical exercise. Peter's response proved they were wrong, and that generosity is more spiritual than we think.

> *Peter said, "Ananias, how did Satan get you to lie to the Holy Spirit and secretly keep back part of the price of the field? Before you sold it, it was all yours, and after you sold it, the money was yours to do with as you wished. So what got into you to pull a trick like this? <u>You didn't lie to men but to God.</u>"*
>
> *Ananias, when he heard those words, fell down dead. That put the fear of God into everyone who heard of it. (Acts 5:3-5, MSG)*

When we live generous lives, we must understand we are not just giving of our resources, time or convenience. We are giving spirit and life to someone else. God is interested in that. As surely as God is interested in stirring your heart, He is equally interested in seeing you take on the business of stirring other hearts.

GENEROSITY IS FROM OVERFLOW

No story proves generosity is spiritual like the story of Zacchaeus. This short man met Jesus and didn't keep it to himself.

In Luke 19, Jesus is making His way through Jericho and Zacchaeus hears about it. Due to vertical physical challenges—he was short—he ran ahead and climbed a sycamore-fig tree to catch a glimpse of the great Rabbi. Zacchaeus could never have guessed what happened when he finally locked eyes with Jesus. Jesus invited himself over to dinner.

This dinner invitation would have been acceptable if Zacchaeus had been a Pharisee or church leader. It would have seemed consistent with the message Jesus came bearing. But here was a sinner of the first order. Zacchaeus was not liked at all! He made his wealth defrauding people during tax season. He was wealthy, short, and had no friends. But here he was, scrambling down the tree to an invitation no one had anticipated. There was a great outcry. How could the Spiritual Teacher eat—or spend any time—with this wicked man? The people saw an abomination, but somewhere in Jericho, a widowed mother who had been defrauded by Zacchaeus was praying for a way to feed her hungry children, and God was about to start a domino effect of generosity that would provide for her!

I assume the most important part of Jesus' visit took place during or after the meal.

> *Meanwhile, Zacchaeus stood before the Lord and said, "I will give half my wealth to the poor, Lord, and if I have cheated people on their taxes, I will give them back four times as much!"*
>
> *Jesus responded, "Salvation has come to this home today, for this man has shown himself to be a true son of Abraham. For the Son of Man came to seek and save those who are lost." (Luke 19:8-10, NLT)*

This man encountered Jesus, and his life was changed forever. And without instruction, he is compelled to be generous. Herein lies the difference between philanthropy and generosity.

PHILANTHROPY VS. GENEROSITY

I will get back to Zacchaeus' story, but I thought I should share this quick thought with you.

Even though generosity and philanthropy are used interchangeably, I believe that they ring very different bells—to a large extent.

Philanthropy, etymologically, is the combination of *philos*

(Greek for "loving") and *anthropos* (Greek for "human being"). Philanthropy focuses on the human condition, the needs, and plight we face as a race and people. It could be in the form of giving towards seeking the cure for a disease, championing a social cause or funding research and advancement in a field that pushes us forward as a global village. An excellent example of this would be Microsoft donating more than $3 Billion in cash and software to bring technology to people who wouldn't get it any way else, thus bridging the global digital divide. With every single dollar or initiative in this package, they advanced the human race as a whole. Philanthropy in its purest form is humanitarian, with most of the energy and resource used to push us forward as a group.

Another word that comes to mind is *charity*. If we are frank with ourselves, we have relegated charity to dropping off used clothes and shoes in a bin outside a mall or office complex, helping out in a soup kitchen on the weekends, giving out coats to the homeless during winter—and when we go really big— sending money to Africa to provide clean water or meals for children. The online version of the Merriam-Webster dictionary defines charity as *"the act of giving money, food, or other kinds of help to people who are poor, sick, etc.."* While philanthropy will fund the development of 2,000 corn farms, a charity will provide meals for the week. Acts of charity will give out fishes while philanthropy will dig new ponds and teach us how to fish.

Sometimes, I feel churches and Christians have resorted to

philanthropy and acts of charity, neglecting the most important thing: reaching the spirit. We have come up with Christian terms for meeting needs without reaching the spirit: Missions and Outreach. Don't get me wrong! God can use philanthropy and charity (in its postmodern definition), but true generosity is a more potent tool.

While philanthropy and charity provide infrastructure and resources for a broken and pitied human state, generosity provides resources in a context that points and leads back to the Source, God. True generosity, the type I cover in this book, is a product of a stirred spirit. The God-kind of generosity is one that sees one stirred spirit seeking out other spirits to stir.

Philanthropy and charity can turn to spiritual generosity when the spirit of the person reached is ignited with the same fire that fuels your spirit. A well is just a source of portable drinking water until it means something to the spirit of the drinker. Until our generosity leads to people becoming Christ-followers, we have not achieved its true goal. Jesus fed the people and they followed him. Jesus healed people, they followed him. Until God has been shared, generosity has not taken place.

ZACCHAEUS' SPIRIT IS STIRRED

Back to Zacchaeus.

Jesus caused an outrage when He chose where He was going to eat dinner that evening. More than half of the crowd thought there were better people—more righteous people—

Jesus could have spent His time with. But today was the day this Zacchaeus's life was going to change forever.

A few hours with Jesus and Zacchaeus had an announcement to make. I can imagine him climbing on the dinner table—he was short—clicking his wine glass, drawing evil glances from everyone, but Jesus. Jesus must have known what he was about to say. This crowd was about to be shocked.

Zacchaeus, standing on that dinner table, announced his decision to give back four times more than he had taken wrongfully. Nobody told him to do so. Jesus didn't suggest this to him. You might see this as restitution, but I beg to differ. Up to this point, he owned what he took, by hook or crook. But something in him had changed. Some force was drawing him to live this new life he had found. Nobody was whispering in his ears, but he could hear it loud and clear: Share some of what you have received! I believe this was just the first step in his generosity journey. What started as a rough evening for a tax collector, grew into dinner with the great Rabbi, and now he couldn't help but share what joy he had found. His spirit was stirred and was overflowing with goodness! His overflow was part of the domino effect that provided for the widow who was praying for a way to feed her hungry children [7].

Generosity cannot be relegated to just giving—something we do either because we have been told to, or we want to justify or silence the voice of selfishness that resides in every one of

---

[7] Permit my hyperactive mind. There is no widow in the Biblical account of this story, but I am guessing some people on Zacchaeus' list got the money they had been praying for.

us. Generosity has to come from overflow. Generosity is an expression of an uncontainable measure of Gods grace in your life. Zacchaeus experienced the grace of God and it filled him to overflow. He had to do something. Generosity is a force that will not let you live for *me, myself and I!* Generosity compels you to live beyond yourself.

In one of his letters to the Corinthian church, Apostle Paul shares a story that puts a nice bow on the overflowing nature of true generosity.

> *Now, friends, I want to report on the surprising and generous ways in which God is working in the churches in Macedonia province. Fierce troubles came down on the people of those churches, pushing them to the very limit. The trial exposed their true colors: They were incredibly happy, though desperately poor. <u>The pressure triggered something totally unexpected: an outpouring of pure and generous gifts.</u> I was there and saw it for myself. They gave offerings of whatever they could—far more than they could afford!—pleading for the privilege of helping out in the relief of poor Christians.*
>
> *This was totally spontaneous, entirely their own idea, and caught us completely off guard. What explains it was that <u>they had first given themselves unreservedly to God</u>… (2 Corinthians 8:1-5, MSG)*

These people were poor and had every reason to keep what they had, but they *pleaded* to give! Why? They experienced God unreservedly, and it translated into unhindered and equally unreserved generosity. Don't tell me you had a God-experience; I will see it in your relentless desire to share with others.

GENEROSITY IS LOVE IN ACTION

Generosity is not what you do, but the spirit that you do it in. The spirit that fuels generosity is love. Here is how it works. You experience the unconditional love, mercy, grace and faithfulness of God, and it installs an engine in your spirit that drives you to share the love you have received. It feels like spontaneous combustion with love for the people around you. True generosity cannot be contained because it is generated in your spirit.

Generosity—love—hangs you on a cross—Jesus Christ—forces a crown of thorns down your head and pierces your side with a spear. It compels you to do for others what Jesus did for you! Do you see the Domino Effect? Generosity is like fire shut up in your bones which requires you to love—giving comes by natural consequence. Generosity in its truest form is loving—not giving. It's not the action of giving that defines generosity; it is the heart of love that characterizes this lifestyle. God is our perfect example. God is love.

> *This is how much God loved the world: He gave his Son, his one and only Son... (John 3:16, MSG)*

Our generous God loved us so much that He gave his best and only Son. His love for us overflowed as generosity towards us. Someone once said, 'Show me your bank statement and I will tell you what you really love.' I believe that we will not unlock the full potential of generosity unless we stop relegating missions and outreaches to just dollar bills, child sponsorships, and missions trips, and not a heart overflowing with love.

Still speaking to Corinthian church, Paul says this:

> *I am not saying this as a command (to dictate to you), but to prove, by (pointing out) the enthusiasm of others, the sincerity of your love as well. (2 Corinthians 8:8, AMP)*

The sincerity of our love can be measured by our generosity. I think my son, Joel, cemented this spiritual lesson in my heart.

When he was younger, Joel held onto everything he hands could grab. You were better served to forget anything his little hands gripped. It was his, and no one was taking it away from him. Everything was his. My couch was his. My clothes and shoes were his. My plate was his. Even my food was somehow his because he was sitting at the table with me. My phone was his (His mom suffered that more). I was 'my daddy' and my wife was 'my mummy'. Like his toys, we belonged to him. He was not willing to share with anyone. To pull his legs, our friends would say we were their dad and mom, and Joel would lose it!

I remember one time he fought off a boy three years older than him for sitting on his bike. On one hand, I was proud that my boy could stand up for himself in a fight (I'm a man's man; don't blame me). But on the other hand, I had to teach him how to share. All our efforts proved futile. But something strange happened sooner rather than later. In the same month

Joel began to say, 'I love you,' he started to become freer with his toys. He didn't mind sharing. He didn't correct us when we claimed what was indeed ours. The love in his heart had grown and was overflowing with generosity.

> *"It's not how much we give but how much love we put into giving." (Mother Teresa)*

THE EFFECTS OF THE SPIRIT OF GENEROSITY

I believe the overflowing spirit of generosity has four effects.

It Compels You

When you have a life-changing encounter with God, you really can't keep it to yourself. You will seek out any opportunities to share it. Overwhelmed by the spirit of generosity, a pay raise doesn't mean new clothes. It means you have more to give. Recently, I gave a laptop to a friend. It was the second I was giving out. I was in the room when he shared the story of how his laptop had been stolen, and before I could think, my mouth opened, and I promised him mine. Generosity compels you to share what you have received. It's unstoppable! It's untamable!

It Sensitizes You

Some months ago, I noticed a member of our church was rotating between three shoes at the most. I don't know how I came about this, but that's what the spirit of generosity does. When you operate in overflowing generosity, your spirit is sensitive to the needs that are not apparent to a regular observer. I gave him one of my boots, and you could have sworn he had prayed for some new shoes. The physical and practical manifestation of my overflowing spirit was an answer to his prayers.

It Encourages You

Sometimes, it is not easy to give, especially when you could use the extra. In Paul's example to the Corinthian church, he makes it a point to explain that the Macedonian church was not giving because they had everything they needed and more. In fact, they had fallen on hard times themselves. When we are torn and struggling, the spirit of generosity encourages us to leave the tap open, because in meeting the needs of others, God meets ours. God is faithful like that.

It Inspires You

Recently, I came up with what I call *Creative Generosity*. When we operate in the true spirit of generosity, we get unique ideas. At one of the Back To School events our church held, I noticed this lady standing close to the line, but not necessarily in it. The spirit of generosity sensitized me to her. I walked up to her and immediately I could perceive she was ashamed she needed the help for her kids but was desperate enough to make it to the event. This lady was on the brink of walking away and missing out on something she needed. I had to get creative. I walked her back to the space shared by our volunteers and gave her a t-shirt. Wearing that t-shirt killed the shame—she was a part of us—and it opened her to receive what we knew would bless her and her kids. Guess what she did after she received her bags filled with school supplies. She stayed behind and served with the rest of the team! The domino effect is one stirred spirit reaching out to another spirit.

The greatest appreciation for what you have received is sharing with the people around you. When we receive grace, we should overflow with grace to other people. When we are recipients of God's unconditional love, it should drive us to love others with the God-kind of love. And when we are blessed with material resources, the same dynamic should play out. Generosity is reaching out with what you have received.

chapter 4

JESUS AND MONEY

For your heart will always be where your riches are.[8]

Money is our most material currency on the earth. We are paid with money. We pay our mortgage and car notes with it. We buy clothes, food, and electronics with it. We support God's work on earth with it too. Money is a very dominant part of our lives as humans. It then should not be surprising that, during His time on earth, Jesus talked about money. In fact, He taught about money more than He did heaven and hell put together. The only subject He talked about more than money was the Kingdom of God. 11 of the 39 parables Jesus taught with were about money and wealth. The Bible has well over 2000 verses that deal with money, wealth, greed, contentment and other

---

[8] *Luke 12:34, GNT*

money-relevant themes. Money-talk was important to Jesus.

Many of us talk, pray and strategize about *getting* money. But we usually don't expend nearly as much energy or develop as much strategy on *giving* it. And when we do our research and seek out more knowledge on money management, it's usually about how best we can keep or multiply what we have. I don't fault this, but if we are sincere with ourselves, selfishness lurks behind most of our financial decisions. We buy the clothes we like. We go to the restaurants we love. We accept the job offers and positions we think best suit us and our needs, and so on. And when we give, it's because it makes us look and (or) feel good. It's usually about what we want and how we want to feel. It's almost always about taking care of number one.

I think that Jesus talked so much about money because He knew we would need a lot of wisdom to help us manage it and our attachment to it. Here're some other reasons I think Jesus thought money-talk was important.

1. Money Influences Your Worship

You can't worship two gods at once. Loving one god, you'll end up hating the other. Adoration of one feeds contempt for the other. <u>You can't worship God and Money both.</u> (Matthew 6:24, MSG)

Our interaction with money exposes the motivation of our hearts, our love, our desires, and most importantly, our worship. Worship? Yes. Money is the only thing Jesus actually acknowledges as competition with God for our worship.

In the text above, money is personified. It is given a personality strong enough to be worshipped—in the place of God. That is because money has a spirit, Mammon, that promises to reward confidence in wealth. Jesus refers to money as a 'god'. Anything done in the worship of any one of the two personalities—money or God—diminishes our adoration of the other. God's chief competition for your heart is locked away in your bank account, or worse still, lost in your sofa.

So how do we worship money? Earlier translations of the Bible use *serve* in place of *worship* in the text above. The Greek meaning of the word is *to obey, to give up one's self*. We serve money when we are willing to adjust our entire lives because of our desire for more money. When money decides your priorities, you're serving money. When the pursuit of money compromises your worship of God—in any way—you have chosen your god. When money or your attachment to it triggers destructive emotions and attitudes, you worship at the altar of money. When you are willing to lose anything to keep or make more money, you are a money-worshipper.

Sidebar. I hope this is politically correct. I apologize if it isn't. Have you ever wondered why Christians in relatively poorer countries of the world have a deeper culture of worship than those from presumably richer nations? Need facilitates dependence. And when all fails, that dependence is placed wholly on God. People who need more, pray more, trust more and worship more. Even though this is usually the case, I have never been an advocate of a need-based relationship with God because when the need is met, dependence wanes. The best relationship with God is not predicated on needs, but a yearning to experience God in all His glory.

We must let our worship and journey with God decide our interaction and attachment to money. God must be the singular object of our affection and worship. This is a higher dimension of living we must strive for.

Worship the Lord your God and only the Lord your God. Serve him with absolute single-heartedness. (Luke 4:8, MSG)

2. Money Reveals Our Heart's Position

For your heart will always be where your riches are. (Luke 12:34, GNT)

Some days ago, while Joel, my son, was eating a lollipop, I asked him to drop it, go upstairs to his room, and get a pair of shoes. He was quite hesitant. Before he made any moves, he made sure to find a clean, safe resting place for his lollipop. I offered to hold onto it for him. You would have thought I asked him to rip his heart out. He reluctantly took me up on my offer. I could see the distrust in his eyes. He was conflicted. Was he supposed to trust me with his prized possession? How was he sure I wouldn't eat it, or worse, dispose of it before he returned?

With every step he took up the stairs, his desperation increased. And when he made the turn on the stairs, I heard him scramble hurriedly to his room, and in seconds he was sliding back down the stairs, shoes in hand. You should have seen the relief in his eyes when he returned to find everything was as he had left it.

To Joel, that lollipop was gold, diamonds, and every precious metal. Even though his body was separated from the candy on a stick, his spirit, mind and soul were holding on for dear life. Joel exemplified what Jesus meant when He taught that your heart is exactly where your treasure is. Whatever you treasure holds your heart captive. If money is at the center of your life—you work, live and compromise for it—I can argue that your heart is tucked away in your wallet, piggy bank, or investment portfolio.

> *Don't hoard treasure down here where it gets eaten by moths and corroded by rust or—worse!—stolen by burglars. Stockpile treasure in heaven, where it's safe from moth and rust and burglars. (Matthew 6:19-20, MSG)*

This doesn't mean you cannot have a bank account or a buoyant retirement portfolio. It simply means those things—money and material possessions—should not be treasured nearly as much as your relationship with Jesus and the implications of it, generous living inclusive. Wealth is fickle. It is here one day and gone the next. You have a job today and tomorrow you're filling applications. We cannot make something as volatile as money the rudder that steers our ships.

I sincerely think we all need a heart-check. It is high time we considered what we treasure the most. Do you have your priorities straight? If not, it is time for a heart-realignment. Anchor your heart where it should be: locked away, securely, with Jesus Christ. And if you tell me your pursuit of money is driven by a fear of not having enough, you have revealed where you trust God the least. In your fear and anxiety, you prove that you trust what the devil says about you more than you believe what God promises. Fear and anxiety never produce the best God wants for us.

3. Money Can Hinder Our Spiritual Growth

To be clear, money is not bad. Handled right, it can enhance your life and your journey with God. It is an inordinate attachment to money that can stunt, or possibly destroy, your spiritual maturity.

In Matthew 19:16, we read the story of a man who approached Jesus seeking the next steps in his spiritual journey. He approached Jesus with some flattery and bragged about how awesome he was at keeping the commandments—I thought he sounded a bit proud, but that's just my opinion. And just when he thought he was the perfect saint, Jesus hit him straight at his heart.

> *"If you want to give it all you've got," Jesus replied, "go sell your possessions; give everything to the poor. All your wealth will then be in heaven. Then come follow me." (Matthew 19:21, MSG)*

The lesson here is not living a life of poverty. Jesus was not asking this man to live a life of destitution. He was gauging this man's attachment to his material wealth.

I have been a pastor and preacher long enough to anticipate certain reactions to money-talk in church. You can teach and preach about any other topic and get a good *Amen* and *Hallelujah* (Halleluya or Alleluia, trying to be religiously correct). Drop the M-word and the best of Christians tense up, holding on a little tighter to their handbags and sitting heavier on their wallets. People have literally walked out on sermons that remotely touched on money. It's a sensitive matter. I get it.

It's easier for us as Christians to give our time and talents, but just don't ask us about our money (treasure). Why are we so apprehensive about a topic Jesus talked about more than He did about heaven or hell? Why do our walls go up? It's also no surprise that one of the highest points of tension in Christian theology is about tithing (money, again).

I think it is high time we accepted that the way we interact with our finances and wealth is a direct indicator of our spiritual maturity. If Jesus spent time talking about a subject, I am pretty sure it plays a significant role in our spirituality. Truly mature Christians handle money with godly wisdom. This wisdom creates financial order—knows where every dollar goes. God blesses order. This godly wisdom also helps to delineate what is ours and what we have been blessed to bless others with. Our spiritual maturity is not measured by how much we have, but by how well we interact with what we have.

The young ruler in the text was presented with his next spiritual steps—generosity and absolute dependence on God—and your guess of his choice is as good as mine.

> *Jesus answered him, "If you wish to be perfect (that is, have the spiritual maturity that accompanies godly character with no moral or ethical deficiencies), go and sell what you have and <u>give (the money) to the poor</u>, and you will have treasure in heaven; and come, <u>follow Me</u> (becoming My disciple, believing and trusting in Me and walking the same path of life that I walk)."*
>
> *But when the young man heard this, he left grieving and distressed, <u>for he owned much property and had many possessions (which he treasured more than his relationship with God)</u>. (Matthew 19:21-22, AMP)*

This man was faced with two choices: eternal life (v.16) or his money, and he chose money. That is how powerful our attachment to money can be. Don't jump down his throat just yet. Anytime you bought that cup of coffee after ignoring the homeless man you noticed at the traffic light; you chose money over eternal life. Anytime you saved up your paid time off from work for vacation, but couldn't spend one day serving the less-served in your community; you chose money over eternal life. If you are inordinately attached to your earthly wealth, it restrains you from opportunities that can further your spiritual journey.

I rest my case with the parable of the sower whose seed fell on four different kinds of soil. The states of the soil in the story parallel the conditions of our hearts whenever we hear the word of God. The seed of the word of God cannot grow in a heart that is money-centric. Here is what happens when the seed of the word of God falls on the soil of a heart of a man or woman driven by a quest for money.

> *The thorny ground represents the hearts of people who listen to the Good News and receive it, but all too quickly the attractions of this world and the delights of wealth, <u>and the search for success and lure of nice things come in and crowd out God's message from their hearts,</u> so that no crop is produced.*
> *(Mark 4:18-19, TLB)*

4. Money Leads To All Kinds Of Evil

An inordinate interaction with money doesn't just stunt your spiritual growth; it fosters the perfect environment for all kinds of evil. While some Christian denominations have made a doctrine of poverty, I think the real doctrine should be founded on how we relate with what we have been blessed with. A wrong alignment with money leads to wrong desires for money and wrong motives for actions.

> *For men who set their hearts on being wealthy <u>expose themselves to temptation</u>. They fall into one of the world's traps, and lay themselves <u>open to all sorts of silly and wicked desires</u>, which are quite capable of utterly ruining and destroying their souls. For <u>loving money leads to all kinds of evil</u>, and some men in the struggle to be rich have lost their faith and caused themselves untold agonies of mind. (1 Timothy 6:9-10, PHILLIPS)*

Own money, control it, spend it, give it, invest it, but don't love it or what it brings. For it is in the love of money, and the consequent, consuming pursuit of it, that we expose ourselves to all sorts of temptation and evil. My heart breaks whenever people tell me they can't be in church anymore because of their job requirements, especially when I know they have options that could lead to a different decision.

I think this point is an extension of the preceding points. If money has your heart and your worship, your spiritual growth is hindered. The further away you are from the heart of God, the easier it is to fall for the temptations loving money brings. And before you know it, you walk away, chasing money—choosing it over your faith and eternal life.

> ... *and some men in the struggle to be rich have lost their faith... (1 Timothy 6:10, PHILLIPS)*

We must not let our attachment to the gift destroy our relationship with the Giver of gifts. We should not give God the terrible responsibility of choosing to withhold His blessings from us because He knows it will tear us away from Him.

5. Money Is A Trust-Test

Not many of us check the integrity of the chairs we sit on before we trust them with all of our weight. For a season of my life, I couldn't help but check to make sure the chair was sturdy before I sat in it.

I was late for a meeting sometime ago and tried the

pretend-you-don't-see-me-enter thing. I snuck into the room and made my way to the nearest chair, like you're supposed to, and *boom shakalaka*! The cookie crumbled, and I was left sprawling on the floor (*Sprawl: to fall with one's arms and legs spread out in an ungainly or awkward way.*[9] I wanted to make sure you got the whole picture). It was one of the most disgraceful moments of my life. The chair had given out on me! My whole act was ruined. My self-worth took a big hit. The meeting became a laugh-fest, and I was the village clown. I got up to my feet with what was left of my dignity and pride, and for months, I made sure it never happened again. (You better not be laughing!)

Experience is a great teacher. What has happened in the past plays a big role in what we allow in the future. The same principle applies to our management of money. How we handle what money we have now greatly determines the extent of our consequent blessing. Mismanage what you have now and you lose the right to ask for more.

> *If you are faithful in little things, you will be faithful in large ones. But if you are dishonest in little things, you won't be honest with greater responsibilities. And if you are untrustworthy about worldly wealth, who will trust you with the true riches of heaven? And if you are not faithful with other people's things, why should you be trusted with things of your own? (Luke 16:10-12, NLT)*

God cannot release you to a higher dimension of financial

---

[9] via www.google.com

blessing and responsibility until you pass the test this level presents. When it comes to money, faithfulness is the currency we trade in. I discuss this later.

Generosity is about love, but it is also about faithfulness. Generosity is essentially giving what came to you but was designated to go through you. And if we are faithful with *other peoples things*, we can be trusted with ours. If you cannot be faithful with *other people's things*, why should you be trusted with yours? A portion of all you receive was designed to go through you to someone else. Do you see where this is going? Generosity positions you to pass the money trust-test that releases you to greater financial blessing and responsibility.

On another note, our management of our earthly wealth greatly determines the extent of our spiritual wealth and relevance. If we are unfaithful with wealth that can be lost, we cannot be trusted with the responsibility of making significant eternal impact. The greatest spiritual wealth (*true riches of heaven*) is being afforded the opportunity to touch lives in ways that have eternal consequences. Misuse money you can count and you stand the chance to miss out on touching lives in ways you can't compute.

6. Money Is Not Eternal

Finally, I believe Jesus taught about money because money is not eternal and should not be treated as such. We cannot compromise what is eternal for what is fleeting.

When I read about the 1929 Stock Market crash and the

subsequent Great Depression, I can't help but feel terrible for the people who took their lives as a result of the loss. Somehow, these people were convinced that the rapid loss of wealth proved there was nothing more to live for. It is shocking to realize how strong our attachment to money can be. If we are not careful, we could let something that was designed to help us live more convenient lives become the very essence of our lives. Money has a lifespan, and it is short.

Here is what King Solomon, the wisest man who ever lived, had to say about money.

> *We all come to the end of our lives as naked and empty-handed as on the day we were born. We can't take our riches with us. (Ecclesiastes 5:15, NLT)*

Money is not the center of your life and should not be. Your life should be centered around an ever-growing relationship with Jesus. You cannot make what should be a periphery of your life, its center. We leave this world as money-less as we came in. If you didn't bring money with you when you arrived on earth, you're definitely taking none of it with you when you depart (I Timothy 6:7). Even if your casket is filled with money, it is useless for where you're going.

I remember opening an envelope one year after Nigeria had switched out its bank notes and finding what was now old and useless ₦5, ₦10, ₦20 and ₦50 notes. I had forgotten them when I switched out my old notes for new ones. 365 days ago, those notes would have bought me something nice—they would have meant something. But now they were just paper—

a historical artifact. I keep them for the memories they trigger. That's how ephemeral money is. It's like fashion trends—one day it's in and the other day it's out. One minute it holds much value and the other it's lost all value. Our lives must be anchored on He who never changes.

> *But as for me, I trust (confidently) in You and Your greatness, O Lord; I said, "You are my God." (Psalm 31:14, AMP)*

> *Whatever is good and perfect is a gift coming down to us from God our Father, who created all the lights in the heavens. He never changes or casts a shifting shadow. (James 1:17, NLT)*

We must move our anchor from the gift to the Giver of the gifts. Gifts expire—money has an expiry date, it leaves you, or you leave it—but the Giver never changes.

If Jesus thought we needed to learn about money directly from Him, we must take it as seriously as He did. Money is strong enough to compete with God for your heart and worship. We must be vigilant to ensure we put it in its place—a tool for world change and not the center of our lives.

> *After all, we brought nothing with us when we came into the world, and we can't take anything with us when we leave it. (1 Timothy 6:7, NLT)*

section two:

Generosity and Others

***Feel free to post quotes and pictures using the tags #generouscity and @victorehiemere

chapter 5

WE ARE CUSTODIANS, NOT OWNERS

When we die our money, fame, and honors will be meaningless. We own nothing in this world. Everything we think we own is in reality only being loaned to us until we... (Michael Huffington)[10]

In the preceding chapters, I have randomly touched on the subject of this chapter. But as I went on this journey, I decided it merited a chapter of its own.

To understand this next story, you must appreciate some of the dynamics that were in play during my childhood. Growing up, the meats in our meals were like prized diamonds. They were not precious because they were scarce. They were precious because of the order in which we ate the elements of our meals. My brothers and I didn't take a bite of

---

[10] via www.brainyquote.com

our meats until every bite of the other elements of our food was gone. No matter how much food was on our plates, we ate our meats last. This led our little minds to appropriated exaggerated amounts of value to those proteinaceous chunks of goodness. To us, the meat was the seal of conclusion. It was the final act before we drank our glasses of water, and got up from the table.

I can't remember exactly, but I think the universally accepted age then was 13. At this age, you were permitted to decide in what order you ate the different elements of your meals. I remember reaching this hallmark before any of my siblings and watching jealousy well up in their eyes as I ate my meats immediately I got my food. What was permissible for me was still an abomination for them. The good ol' days!

One night, while my mother made one of her legendary stews, I walked in on an incredible proposition. She offered me three beef chunks, one for me and one piece for each of my two brothers. I am the first of three boys and a girl (She was not on the scene yet). I could swear I left the kitchen with a hop and a skip in my step. About 25 steps from the bedroom, temptation arose. The aroma of the stew had filled my lungs and had begun giving my brain naughty ideas. My brothers didn't know I had these precious gifts. They wouldn't miss what they never knew existed. My mother would not know they didn't receive it if they never bought it up, and they would never bring it up because they would never know it existed—I can see loopholes in my plan now. And yes, I fell for the temptation.

I made a quick detour to the bathroom, sat on the edge of

the bathtub, and devoured those three chunks of awesome goodness. My mom is a great cook; so you can imagine my immense euphoria. Every bite took me closer to heaven. With the last bite, I could have sworn I saw the face of God! Five minutes later, I was glowing with satisfaction as I opened that bathroom door. My heart was full, and I couldn't help the broad smile that adorned my face.

Fast forward two hours later, during dinner, someone made a reference to meats and my heart sunk. My mother immediately remembered her gifts to us and rebuked my brothers for not expressing their gratitude. They were confused, to say the least. When the anxious trade of words was over, the silence revealed the culprit. My secret was out! My beautifully laid plan had failed me. My euphoria quickly dissipated. My brothers gave me the stink eyes, and I could see I had lost some trust with my mom. I had to be punished for this atrocity. I had to pay for my sins—at least that's what my brothers solicited should happen.

Till this day, I think my punishment was unfair. I was sentenced to one week of meatless meals. During this time, my brothers were going to get a double portion. 21 meatless meals were no joke to a young me! I don't think I have a single vegan bone in my body. I just don't think I have the discipline for that life. I love meat! This was 21 missed opportunities! It was overwhelming to my young mind. I ate two pieces of meat meant for my brothers and lost out on 21 pieces that could have been mine. Suddenly, what had been an ecstatic experience turned to pebbles in my mouth. I fell back on my dietary protein supply doing those days—and I still haven't made it up. At 5' 11", I blame that week for the one inch that would have pushed me to a straight 6'. I'm still paying for my sins! Just kidding.

On a serious note though, I was placed in charge of the resources allocated to my brothers and me, and I spent it all on myself. Herein lies the challenge this chapter poses: How many of us have assumed that all we have received belongs to us? How many of us have gulped down everything in our cups, including what was meant for others? How many of us are guilty of misappropriating the blessings or resources we have received?

OUR RESOURCE HAS A SOURCE

Let's do a quick Bible study.

> *If you start thinking to yourselves, "I did all this. And all by myself. I'm rich. It's all mine!"—well, think again. Remember that God, your God, gave you the strength to produce all this wealth so as to confirm the covenant that he promised to your ancestors—as it is today. (Deuteronomy 8:17-18, MSG)*

> *And he blessed him and said: "Blessed be Abram of God Most High, possessor of heaven and earth… (Genesis 14:19, NKJV)*

> *The earth is the Lord's, and everything in it. The world and all its people belong to him. (Psalm 24:1, NLT)*

> *For all the animals of the forest are mine, and I own the cattle on a thousand hills. If I were hungry, I would not tell you, for all the world is mine and everything in it. (Psalm 50:10, 12, NLT)*

> *O Lord, how manifold are Your works! In wisdom You have made them all. <u>The earth is full of Your possessions.</u> (Psalm 104:24, NKJV)*

> *The silver is mine, and the gold is mine, says the Lord of Heaven's Armies. (Haggai 2:8, NLT)*

Do you notice the recurring theme? If you missed it, here it is: The heavens, the earth, and everything we see belong to God. He is the possessor of the heavens and the earth.

While money remains a difficult subject to broach, we must acknowledge and accept the truth that our resources come from a source. That source is God. God doesn't just own everything; He gives us the power to make wealth (Deuteronomy 8:17-18). And if our resources—and the power to get them—come from God, it is reasonable to appreciate that what ever He blesses us with has a pre-destined assignment it must fulfill.

In the preceding chapters, we learnt that some of all that comes to you, comes for you, and the rest of it comes through you. The three chunks of meat I received had a clear pre-determined assignment. On of my good pastor-friends, Larry Mack, puts it this way, *"Every blessing has an instruction attached to it. And we never unlock the fullest potential of the blessing until the accompanying instruction is carried out to the latter."* The first blessing recorded in the Bible came with an instruction

(Genesis 1:28). When God called out and blessed Abraham, He also gave a set of instructions.

And I will make you a great nation, And I will bless you, And make your name great; And so you shall be a blessing; And I will bless those who bless you, And the one who curses you I will curse. And in you all the families of the earth will be blessed. (Genesis 12:2-3, NASB. Emphasis, mine)

Look at it this way. Every blessing you receive comes wrapped up with responsibility. It shifts generosity from a because-I-was-told-to realm to a because-I-get-to realm. When you get that raise, you get the greater responsibility to reach more people.

Great gifts mean great <u>responsibilities</u>; greater gifts, greater <u>responsibilities</u>! (Luke 12:48, MSG)

In the story of the rich fool in Luke 12, God blesses him with a bountiful harvest, and we see this rich man make the biggest resource-mistake there is. His actions prove he didn't understand that all that came to him was not all for him. His selfishness inspired him to tear down what was a functioning and adequate barn and build a bigger one. The agenda for this new barn was clear: store ALL of the harvest that came to him. In the end, the rich man died because, just like I did with those chunks of meat my mom gave me, he interacted with his resources like an owner when he was a mere custodian. It is this custodian-posture that I explore in this chapter.

THE POSTURE OF ENGAGEMENT

Another parable precedes the parable of talents in Matthew 25. Both of these parables explore what our postures as Christians should be. The Parable of the Ten Virgins (Matthew 25:1-13) speaks to a *posture of expectation and readiness*. In the story, ten virgins wait on the arrival of the groom. The wait takes longer than anticipated, and they all fall asleep. The groom finally arrives and only five of the virgins are ready for the wedding banquet. The other five were locked out of the room altogether. Here is the moral of the story: We must live lives that look forward to a glorious eternity. This world is not all there is; neither is it the end.

From verse 14, we begin to explore a *posture of engagement*. While we expect an eternity with God, we must engage our world and the people in it in our everyday life. In engaging our community and the world, we reach more people with the love of Jesus. Let's look at Jesus' teaching on engagement.

> *"For it is as if a man, going on a journey, summoned his slaves and entrusted his property to them; to one he gave five talents, to another two, to another one, to each according to his ability. Then he went away. The one who had received the five talents went off at once and traded with them, and made five more talents. In the same way, the one who had the two talents made two more talents. But the one who had received the one talent went off and dug a hole in the ground and hid his master's money. After a long time the master of those slaves came and settled accounts with them. (Matthew 25:14-19, NRSV)*

You can find Luke's version of this story in Luke 19:11-27. But before we go on to the rest of this story, let's examine a major dynamic of this parable.

Over the years, *talent* in this story has been taught to mean many things including skills or gifts (talents), opportunities and money. The Greek word, *talanton*, is defined as *a certain weight or scale of balance*. This scale of balance was used to measure currency for trade or exchange. It was different state to state, or varied according to the changes in the laws regulating currency. Any way you look at it, *talent* (or *talanton*) is currency—in most cases, precious stones like silver or gold.

Here are other reasons I think *talent* in our story is money.

- *It could be invested or traded with (Matthew 25:16, Luke 19:16)*
- *It could yield an interest (Matthew 25:16, Luke 19:16)*
- *It could be banked (Matthew 25:27, Luke 19:23)*
- *It only yielded interests when it was banked or traded with*
- *It must be accounted for*
- *Faithfulness or unfaithfulness with it positions us for more, or denies us of what we already have or could receive (Matthew 25:20-30)*

All of the above-listed qualities point to finances more than they do any other themes. God is extremely interested in what we do with what He blesses us with. Our resources are mission-critical. They are mission tools. With our resources, we do business for God on the earth. With our resources, we engage our communities for God. We are brokers for the Kingdom of God. We make investments in the lives of people, and these investments prompt them to turn to God.

Your money and every other resource you have been blessed with is seed-money for God's business in and through you. Just like the easiest way to kill a business in its infantile stage is to misappropriate the seed-money, the easiest way to stunt what God can do in your community through you is mishandling what you have been made responsible for. Our selfishness can stop a Domino Effect that has the potential to point thousands of people to the freeing grace of Jesus.

The Luke 19 version of this story begins with revealing the purpose of this lesson. In verse Luke 19:11, Jesus had to correct a false impression that the people had. They followed Jesus, and watching him go into Jerusalem, they"... *thought that the kingdom of God was going to appear at once."* (Luke 19:11, NIV). The Kingdom of God is not an instantaneous phenomenon. The power of the Kingdom of God is revealed, unleashed and multiplied when every citizen of this Kingdom plays their part in God's Domino Effect.

Until we, as custodians, make the shift and interact with our resources like God intends, we will not realize the power to change the world that we have. It is on this premise that Jesus shares this parable.

chapter 6

MOLDS OF CUSTODIANS

"Being generous often consists of simply extending a hand. That's hard to do if you are grasping tightly..." [11]

A custodian is a person who is responsible for or looks after something placed in his or her charge. In Matthew's account of the Parable of the Talents, the story begins with a nobleman placing some currency in the charge of his servants. He made them custodians of his resources (Matthew 25:14). But Luke's version uses a word that sheds light on what the master intended for his servants.

He said therefore, A certain nobleman went into a far country to receive for himself a kingdom, and to return. And he called his

---

[11] Digh, P. (2008). *Life is a verb: 37 days to wake up, be mindful, and live intentionally.* Guilford, CT: Skirt.

ten servants, and delivered them ten pounds, and said unto them, Occupy till I come. (Luke 19:12-13, KJV)

The word *occupy* is translated from the Greek word *pragmateuomai*. It means *to be occupied in anything or to carry on the business of a banker or a trader*. The heart of this word can be seen in Bible translations that render *occupy* as *'Do business'* or *'Invest.'* As Christ-followers and citizens of His Kingdom, we have been called to the business of investing. True generosity is doing business for God. That is what *occupying* looks like.

God is a venture capitalist. He invests in the business of filling the earth with the knowledge of His glory (Habakkuk 2:14). And the resources we receive from Him serve as seed money; they are investments we must make in the lives of the people around us. Your resources are one of the vehicles that deliver your divine purpose. When God blesses you, it usually comes packed with what you should busy yourself with. Your divine business—purpose—is wrapped up in the blessings you receive.

In the meaning of *occupy*, we are introduced to two of the three molds of custodians.

FIRST MOLD: BANKER

It must be understood that the mold of a banker was not part of the original instruction or commission. We are introduced to this when the master reprimands one of the servants for taking on a mold that we will discuss later.

6: Molds Of Custodians

> *Then the one who had received the one talent also came forward, saying, 'Master, I knew that you were a harsh man, reaping where you did not sow, and gathering where you did not scatter seed; so I was afraid, and I went and hid your talent in the ground. Here you have what is yours.' But his master replied, 'You wicked and lazy slave! You knew, did you, that I reap where I did not sow, and gather where I did not scatter? Then you ought to have <u>invested my money with the bankers</u>, and on my return <u>I would have received what was my own with interest</u>. (Matthew 25:24-27, NRSV)*

From the parable, it is clear that the custodians mold of banking is considered investing, but at a very elementary level. On this level of investing, you do the barest minimum there is to get a Return On Investment.

In ancient eastern cultures, money-changers would sit at tables in public places, receiving and exchanging currencies from their clients. People would walk up to these money-changers, deposit money, and on an agreed date, withdraw their money with accrued interest based on an agreed rate. It's the same philosophy that governs Fixed or Time Deposits. Generally, a certain amount of money is deposited with the bank, and on the agreed maturity date, the client withdraws his deposit on the agreed interest rate. Typically, the longer the term of deposit, the higher is the rate of interest.

In this story, Jesus rebuked the servant for not doing the barest minimum. He should have taken the money put in his charge to the *trapeza (the table or stand of a money changer, where he sits, exchanging different kinds of money for a fee, and paying back with interest loans or deposits*). Banking the money would have provided security and interest on the investment with the least effort.

As responsible followers of Christ, this is the mold of a banker looks like for us. Extensive study of the Bible reveals certain expectations and responsibilities as concerns money. The barest minimum includes committing ourselves to financial order, budgeting, and tithing and giving offerings. This is the barest minimum we must do. Financial planning and budgeting help to create and maintain a sense of responsibility and order. Christianity doesn't preclude us from financial intelligence. In fact, it speaks volumes about our commitment to properly managing what God has entrusted to us.

Here are biblical perspectives on some financial management principles.

Proper Accounting

>*Know the state of your flocks, and put your heart into caring for your herds, for riches don't last forever, and the crown might not be passed to the next generation. (Proverbs 27:23-24, NLT)*

To properly manage a thing, you must be able to account for it. As responsible custodians of the resources we have been blessed with, we must be able to keep good accounts. Where is every dollar going? What portion of your budget gets the most of your money? Is your money spent in line with your personal or family mission? Proper accounting requires us to ask ourselves the difficult and necessary questions.

Budgeting

But don't begin until you count the cost. For who would begin construction of a building without first calculating the cost to see if there is enough money to finish it? (Luke 14:28, NLT)

Budgeting goes hand in hand with proper accounting. Without budgets, we leave ourselves vulnerable to financial mishaps and mismanagement. Budgeting takes into account what we have and intentionally pours into whatever mediums we see as priorities.

Sidebar. Over the years, I have seen people make budgets and upon examination, I have failed to see where generosity comes into play. I see a plan for bills to be paid. I see a plan for buoyant savings and investment portfolios. But sometimes, I can't find that provision for picking up that extra cup of coffee for a co-worker, or that extra bag of groceries for the local food pantry.

Our budgets scream what our priorities are. We must be willing to be as intentional about what we spend outside of ourselves as we are with what we spend on ourselves.

Saving

A prudent person <u>foresees danger and takes precautions</u>. The simpleton goes blindly on and suffers the consequences. (Proverbs 22:3, NLT)

> *Take a lesson from the ants, you lazybones. Learn from their ways and become wise! Though they have no prince or governor or ruler to make them work, they labor hard all summer, <u>gathering food for the winter</u>. (Proverbs 6:6-8, NLT)*

Saving is a wise financial strategy. It provides a margin for the unexpected. Our savings can also provide the seed for our financial future.

A pastor-friend of mine once taught me that savings are not just for rainy days or seasons; they can be the advantage when God opens unexpected doors for us. He shared a story of how his church was able to buy a facility at an extremely low cost because they had some money set aside in savings. He told me that they didn't necessarily need the building at that time, but had to make the move because they didn't see that kind of facility ever being priced that low again. And guess what? In three years, when they finally needed to expand, they had what they needed for their next phase as a church. Upon market research, he realized that their financial prudence secured their next season for almost an eighth of the market value.

Savings are not just blankets in cold seasons; they can be the power that propels you into your next season.

Minimal Debts

> *Just as the rich rule the poor, so the borrower is servant to the lender. (Proverbs 22:7, NLT)*

The Bible doesn't command us against borrowing or having debts. It just states what happens when we live in debt.

Whoever we are indebted to, we are subject to. Many of us are paralyzed from moving into our next season because of the debts of this and past seasons. God has called you to make big moves, but the balance on your credit card might be holding you back. God has called you to move to another country, but your bills are saying otherwise. God might have called you to build schools in less served areas of the world, but the poor financial decisions of your past have become a weight that keeps you rooted short of your potential. I believe that the less debt we live in, the freer we are to obey God's leading.

Financial Investments

> *But divide your investments among many places, for you do not know what risks might lie ahead. (Ecclesiastes 11:2, NLT)*

Recently, my wife turned me to a mobile app that facilitates on-the-spot financial investments. It looks interesting. I plan to give it a deeper look in the near future. I sincerely believe that we must be diligent to invest what resources we have in wise financial opportunities. Investments provide viable opportunities to multiply what we have in our hands, and thus, increase our potential to impact our communities for God.

THE TENTH SECURES THE REST

Practicing these principles of financial responsibility positions you to do the best you can to secure and invest what has been placed in your charge. But even at our best, we cannot guarantee the security of the resources we have been blessed with. Somehow, in some way, even though we are caretakers and custodians, we must leave the ultimate responsibility of security to God.

> *Unless the Lord builds the house, they labor in vain who build it; unless the Lord guards the city, the watchman keeps awake in vain. (Psalm 127:1, AMP)*

The one sure way to employ the divine protective services of God over our resources is tithing.

The tithe, *ma'aser*, is the tenth part of a thing—the first tenth. Even though tithing is a controversial facet of Christian theology amongst the varied denominations, it's power cannot be denied.

I subscribe to tithing because, amongst other things, I believe it is a spiritual exercise of sacrificial worship that represents my priorities and understanding that all I am and have belong to God. Tithing is our way of acknowledging and recognizing the Source of our resources. It has the added benefits of security, multiplied blessings, protection, and global and trans-generational blessings. Tithing is God's way of connecting us to His infallible grace over our finances. What is so difficult about bringing back 10% to the One who has blessed you with 100%?

> *Bring all the tithes into the storehouse so there will be enough food in my Temple. If you do," says the Lord of Heaven's Armies, "I will open the windows of heaven for you. I will pour out a*

blessing so great you won't have enough room to take it in! Try it! Put me to the test! Your crops will be abundant, <u>for I will guard them</u> from insects and disease. Your grapes will not fall from the vine before they are ripe," says the Lord of Heaven's Armies. "Then all nations will call you blessed, for your land will be such a delight," says the Lord of Heaven's Armies. (Malachi 3:10-12, NLT)

The banking mold of a custodian is an elementary expression of our posture as custodians of our resources. We cannot make the banker mold the hallmark of our responsibilities as custodians. It would be like assuming you were placed on the earth to inhale Oxygen-saturated air and exhale Carbon-dioxide-saturated air. That is what everyone does. Anyone who recognizes God as the source and true owner is first and foremost a banker—that is the barest minimum. We must, therefore, move on to our true assignment and mold.

THE SECOND MOLD: TRADER

The one who had received the five talents went off at once and <u>traded with them</u>, and made five more talents. In the same way, the one who had the two talents made two more talents. (Matthew 25:16-17, NRSV)

In line with the master's original intent for his servants, the first two servants put their talents to work. The word *trade* translates from a Greek word that means *to toil, labor or work*. When we put the resources we have been blessed with to work we activate the power our resources posses. In the trader mold, we live beyond ourselves. It is on the level—in this custodian mold—that we engage in true generosity.

Even if the two servants who traded came back with double their investments (seed-money), I believe that doubling their monetary values was a representation of reproducing themselves. The five-talent servant came home with another five-talent servant he had influenced, equaling ten talents. Do you see the Domino Effect? I believe that if the master had spent some more time away from home, the two-talents servant might have come back with 20 talents, multiplying himself a whooping ten times! This is what we have been called to do. Use the resources you have been blessed with to point more people to the true Source. And when they encounter the Source, they become a resource to other people!

Moving beyond financial resources, I believe that you and I are resources to our communities. God has positioned and blessed us to pour into the lives of the people He has placed around us. It is in pouring out—generous living—that we pass on this freeing grace that we have experienced.

Trading Means Moving Out

God has called us to trade. Trading means we must put ourselves out there. My uncle is a trader in all kinds of wood. I remember spending some weekends in his house and noticed that, no matter how early I woke up, I never saw him leave for work. He woke up very early every morning to open his business doors. Long before any of his clients woke up he was ready for them.

Trading in God's kingdom means you have to put yourself out there. You cannot sit locked away at home, in the comfort of your friends, family and acquaintances, and claim you are trading. The servant with five talents would not have succeeded in trading if he woke up every morning to a good breakfast, and spent the rest of the day roaming around the house.

Trading means venturing into unknown territories. It means meeting people you have never met before. Trading means going to places you have never gone before. Trading can be an American going to live permanently in Kenya, and it might also mean moving from Nigeria to the Ukraine. It means increasing your circle of influence to increase the influence of God's grace in the world. Compare this line of thought to the Great Commission.

> *But you will receive power when the Holy Spirit comes upon you. And you will be my witnesses, <u>telling people about me everywhere</u>—in Jerusalem, throughout Judea, in Samaria, and to the ends of the earth. (Acts 1:8, NLT)*

If you check out a map of the region, you'll realize that Jerusalem, Judaea and Samaria represent increasing concentric circles of influence. They represent a city-state-nation increasing level of influence. Trading for God will require you to move from a city level to a state level to a national level, and dare I say, a global level.

My pastor, Jimmy Rollins, teaches a great lesson on what it means to reach the *uttermost parts of the earth* (the way the King James Version renders *"..ends of the earth"* in Acts 1:8). In this lesson, Pastor Jimmy basis the heart of our commission to reach the ends of the world on the Greek word translated as uttermost, *Eschatos*. *Eschatos* means *last in time, rank, and place*. God has called us to reach beyond our comfort zones, spiritual uniformity and conformity, to the people we would naturally spend the least amount of time with, and the people and places we would naturally consider the last on our list. *Trading* means going out to everywhere, investing in everyone. No preferences.

Trading Means Strategic Positioning

Every trader understands the advantage of right positioning. Whether it is physical or virtual, ranging from the perfect sign over a store front office to an awesome web banner, great businesses strive to put themselves in front of people if they hope to drum up any patronage.

Check this out.

> *You are the light of the world—like a city on a hilltop that cannot be hidden. <u>No one lights a lamp and then puts it under a basket. Instead, a lamp is placed on a stand, where it gives light to everyone in the house.</u> In the same way, <u>let your good deeds shine out for all to see</u>, so that everyone will praise your heavenly Father. (Matthew 5:14-16, NLT)*

The master never intended for the servants to hold onto and

remain dormant with the talents they received. God didn't expend His grace on you to enjoy all to yourself. You are light. Shine for all to see! It's time to position yourself to impact the people around you. No one lights a lamp and puts it under a basket. No good custodian receives resources from the Source and holds it back to himself. Get out there. Take your place in your office, at your kids' soccer practice, in that Parent-Teacher meeting. Position yourself for maximal trading—impact—and influence in your community for God.

Trading Entails Risk

God has called us to trade, and the stock we trade in is *people*. And like in a true business sense, even though trading in stocks commands higher interests and multiplies potential seed-money, it is risky.

Growing up, I invested in the shares of a company, and ten years later their value tanked! I lost the value of my investment. But here is the good news, the human stock never goes down. No matter how broken, battered, abused, discombobulated you might be, your stock with God never goes down. A hundred-dollar bill holds its value whether it is torn, wet, crumbled or stepped upon. You are as valuable to God as the day He created you in your mother's womb. Don't let anyone lead you to believe otherwise. You are very valuable; God went all in on you!

<u>For God so (greatly) loved and dearly prized the world</u>, that He (even)gave His (One and) only begotten Son, so that whoever

believes and trusts in Him (as Savior) shall not perish, but have eternal life. (John 3:16, AMP)

<u>You were bought with a price (a precious price paid by Christ)</u>… (1 Corinthians 7:23, AMP)

Look at the ravens. They don't plant or harvest or store food in barns, for God feeds them. And <u>you are far more valuable</u> to him than any birds! (Luke 12:24, NLT)

God risked Jesus to buy you back. That's how valuable you are. It is this value we have been called to remind people of. That is what grace does: it reinstates you to your original relationship with your Father.

There is truly no risk when we trade for God. We might lose our comfort, our agenda, and in some cases our lives, but the interest—the lives we reach for Him—is of unfathomable value!

THE THIRD MOLD: HOARDER

This mold can be seen in Matthew 25:18 and Luke 19:20.

But the one who had received the one talent went off and <u>dug a hole in the ground and hid his master's money.</u> (Matthew 25:18, NRSV)

Then the other came, saying, 'Lord, here is your pound. <u>I wrapped it up in a piece of cloth</u>… (Luke 19:20, NRSV)

I struggled with what to call this mold of custodians. In

Matthew's account, he says the servant buried the talent he received in the earth. In Luke's account, the servant wraps it up in a piece of cloth. In banking and trading, we invest at different levels, yielding varying interests and returns. In burying, we defeat the purpose entirely—there is no Return On Investment! To do this justice, I have decided to discuss this mold in two different modules.

Do Nothing With It

The servant, according to Luke's account of the story decided to do nothing. He didn't trade or bank. He didn't even keep the talent in view, He wrapped it up and decided there was nothing for him to do.

God doesn't bless us for nothing. He blesses us for our pleasure and His pleasure which includes blessing others. Good custodians don't do *nothing*; they invest what they have received to further the mission of their master. This, my friends, is our assignment. Do something with what you have been blessed with. Do something to meet the needs and change the lives around you.

Bury It

Let's do another quick Bible study.

The first man was called Adam. In Genesis 2:7, we see that Adam was made from the dust of the ground (the Hebrew word, *'adamah*). You get it, Adam, the first man, was made from *'adamah*. And when we die, it is said that our bodies return to where it came from, the dust of the ground. Our spirits go back to God.

In the story, the servant decides to bury his talent in the ground (the Greek word, *gē*). Both words, *'adamah* and *gē*, amongst other things, mean *tillable or arable ground.*

Let me bring this all together. When the servant decided to bury the talent he received, he decided to invest it in himself (The *ground* investing in *ground*). Burying the talent in the ground is the spiritual representation of using what you have received only for matters that concern you. When you bury what you have received, there is no room for God in your resources. This is exactly what happens when you withhold your tithe from God or turn a blind eye to the needs around you. You choose to bury your talent in the ground. You choose to be selfish with what you have been blessed with.

When we invest in agendas beyond ourselves, we can be said to be planting. But when we hoard our resources, it dies— buried in our selfishness. When you return your tithe to God and invest in others, you activate the life of God in your resources. When you withhold your resources from God and His agenda, you kill off what power there is in what you have been blessed with.

> *There is the one who (generously) scatters (abroad), and yet increases all the more; and <u>there is the one who withholds what is justly due, but it results only in want and poverty</u>. The generous man (is a source of blessing and) shall be prosperous and enriched, and he who waters will himself be watered (reaping the generosity he has sown). (Proverbs 11:24-25, AMP)*

When we chose to *bury* what we have been blessed with, we reveal that inner toggle between our selfish nature and the will of God. In the third servant's statement to his master, we see his selfishness at war with the truth he was refusing to accept.

> *Then the one who had received the one talent also came forward, saying, 'Master, I knew that you were a harsh man, reaping where you did not sow, and gathering where you did not scatter seed; so I was afraid, and <u>I went and hid your talent</u> in the ground. <u>Here you have what is yours</u>.' (Matthew 25:24-25, NRSV)*

On one hand, he calls his master a harsh man, who wanted interests on investments he didn't make. And on the other hand, he owns up that what he received didn't belong to him in the first place; it belonged to his master.

In his statement, the servant showed that he missed two things. First, whatever you have received from God is an investment in your life. God kicks off the Domino Effect by first investing in us. We continue the chain reaction when we reach and invest in others. Secondly, whatever investments God makes in your life has a purpose to it: *do business, trade*. When we understand that we are businessmen and women, brokers and traders—custodians—of the resources we have been blessed with, we are left with one very important task: stay connected to the Source to learn how the resource is supposed to be appropriated.

Whenever we take on the third mold—hoarding—Jesus

calls us "... *wicked and lazy.*" (Matthew 25:26). Lazy, because we chose to do nothing, and wicked because we chose to reserve all we have received for ourselves.

chapter 7

THE PROFILE OF A CUSTODIAN

A faithful, sensible servant is one to whom the master can give the responsibility of managing his... household... [12]

When you see your relationship with God, and the blessings you receive from Him as an investment—the favor, love, and grace He sheds on you—it compels you to strive to get a return on that invest. The ultimate return on investment in you is other people stirred and pointed to Jesus. Anything short of this is a poor return on investment. Generosity is a potent vehicle that delivers lost and broken people to a God who loves them and died to set them free.

Here is the summary of the matter, and a profile of a faithful custodian.

---

[12] Luke 12:42, NLT

1. Custodians Know God Is The Source

The story in Matthew 25 starts by stating that the talents belonged to the master.

> *For it is as if a man, going on a journey, summoned his slaves and entrusted <u>his property</u> to them. (Matthew 25:14, NRSV)*

Whatever you have or think you have worked to have is a gift from the ultimate Source, God. Somehow, hard work and increased wealth lead us to believe we own what we are blessed with. There are people who work harder than you, but have not been blessed as much as you have. We must not forget that it is God who enables us to make wealth (Deuteronomy 8:17-18).

> *Tell those rich in this world's wealth to quit being so full of themselves and so obsessed with money, which is here today and gone tomorrow. Tell them to go after God, who piles on all the riches we could ever manage—to do good, to be rich in helping others, to be extravagantly generous. If they do that, they'll build a treasury that will last, gaining life that is truly life. (1 Timothy 6:17-19, MSG)*

2. Custodians Understand They Have Varying Abilities And Trust Levels

Some people would lose their minds if they stumbled on $10,000,000. Research shows that a high percentage of lottery winners go broke just years after their winnings.

> *Indeed, 44% of those who have ever won large lottery prizes were broke within five years, according to a 2015 Camelot Group study. The Certified Financial Planner Board of Standards says nearly a third declared bankruptcy—meaning they were worse off than before they became rich. Other studies show that lottery winners frequently become estranged from family and friends, and incur a greater incidence of depression, drug and alcohol abuse, divorce, and suicide than the average American.*[13]

In the story, the master gave out talents according to his perception of the abilities of his servants (Matthew 25:15). It is our responsibility to show God that we can be trusted with more. And there is no better way to show you can be trusted with more than faithfulness with what you have been given.

> *And the Lord replied, "A faithful, sensible servant is one to whom the master can give the responsibility of managing his other household servants and feeding them. If the master returns and finds that the servant has done a good job, there will be a reward. I tell you the truth, the master will put that servant in charge of all he owns. (Luke 12:42-44, NLT)*

3. Custodians Use Resources For The Owner's Purposes

My younger brother, Rhema, owes me for saving his life. While he was in high school, I intercepted a letter he wrote to my dad. Apparently, he had asked my dad for some money and received a not-so-pleasant response. Rhema took a rather interesting stance in his letter. He postulated that if God has

---

[13] via www.fortune.com

gifted him to my mom and dad, God must have also provided for his care. In other words, if my dad was saying there was no money for him—Rhema—my dad was saying he had misappropriated funds earmarked for him by God. My dad would have let him have it if he had seen that letter. Even though I conveyed a watered-down verbal version of the letter, Rhema's claims make some sense.

As custodians, we must realize that whatever we have been made responsible for must be used in the service of the Source. In Matthew 25, the master rewarded the servants who obeyed him. Take a look at 1 Timothy 6 again.

> *Tell those rich in this world's wealth to quit being so full of themselves and so obsessed with money, which is here today and gone tomorrow. Tell them to go after God, who piles on all the riches we could ever manage—<u>to do good, to be rich in helping others, to be extravagantly generous.</u> If they do that, they'll build a treasury that will last, gaining life that is truly life. (1 Timothy 6:17-19, MSG)*

Paul, in his letter to Timothy, explains what the purposes of our resources is: *to do good, to be rich in helping others, to be extravagantly generous.* We deny that God is our source when we use our resources for purposes other than His. Money spent on non-eternal proposes will not trigger eternal benefits, consequences, and rewards.

4. Custodians Know They Will Give An Account

One of the requisites of a custodian is his or her ability to give an account of what has been placed in his or her care. The lesson in the story of the talents is revealed in the servants' account of their business.

> *After a long time the master of those slaves came and settled accounts with them. (Matthew 25:19, NRSV)*

Each of us is going stand before God and give an account of how we interacted with the resources that were placed in our care. Did we bury, hoard, bank or trade with it? Let's be clear: our assignment is to trade. Nothing short of this will make the cut. The spirit of generosity compels and inspires us to trade for God in a world in need of hope, love and grace.

> *Yes, each of us will give a personal account to God. (Romans 14:12, NLT)*

> *For we (believers will be called to account and) must all appear before the judgment seat of Christ, so that each one may be repaid for what has been done in the body, whether good or bad (that is, each will be held responsible for his actions, purposes, goals, motives—<u>the use or misuse of his time, opportunities and abilities</u>). (2 Corinthians 5:10, AMP)*

5. Custodians Enjoy The Benefits Of Faithfulness

The reaction of the master justified the actions each servant took. To the one who hoarded or buried his talent, his unfaithfulness was met with separation and suffering.

> *As for this worthless slave, throw him into the outer darkness, where there will be weeping and gnashing of teeth. (Matthew 25:30, NRSV)*

The other two servants who traded their talents received greater trust and the favor of their master for their faithfulness.

> *And the one with the two talents also came forward, saying, 'Master, you handed over to me two talents; see, I have made two more talents.' His master said to him, 'Well done, good and trustworthy slave; <u>you have been trustworthy in a few things, I will put you in charge of many things; enter into the joy of your master.</u> (Matthew 25:2-23, NRSV)*

As custodians, we trade in faithfulness. In a preceding chapter, we learnt that money is a trust-tester. It tests the condition of our hearts, our motives, and our worship. Our interaction with our resources—especially our money—is important to God because it is the closest representation of the true states of our hearts.

> *If you are faithful in little things, you will be faithful in large ones. But if you are dishonest in little things, you won't be honest with greater responsibilities. And if you are untrustworthy about worldly wealth, who will trust you with the true riches of heaven? (Luke 16:10-11, NLT)*

God responds to our faithfulness. Our faithfulness triggers His trust. The story of the talents ends in a rather interesting manner. In the beginning, it is established that the talents belonged to the master. But never in the story do we see the master take back the talents, except in the case of the servant who buried his talent. In fact, a change of ownership occurred in the end. The faithful servants became owners and rulers like their master.

> *So take the talent away from him, and give it to the one who <u>has</u> the ten talents. For to everyone who has (and values his blessings and gifts from God, and has used them wisely), more will be given, and (he will be richly supplied so that) he will have an abundance... (Matthew 25:28-30, AMP)*

The servants started out trading for their master and ending up owning like the master. The Message translation renders this beautifully.

> *The one given five thousand dollars showed him how he had doubled his investment. His master commended him: 'Good work! You did your job well. <u>From now on be my partner.</u>' (Matthew 25:20-21, MSG)*

God earnestly desires partners who will change the world with and for him. At i5 CHURCH, we never cease to be grateful for the opportunities we have to partner with God to change the world. Partnership with God is obtained through faithfulness. If you are faithful, God will trust you. The more He can trust *through* you, the more He can trust *to* you. If God can trust you to pass on $1,000,000, He surely can trust you to keep that amount too. It is no surprise that it was the servant with now 10 talents that was trusted with the one from the unfaithful servant. The former had the biggest capacity of all the three servants. Increase your capacity to influence the world, and watch God position you to influence more of the world.

God blesses His custodians. He rewards them with ownership because He knows that even as owners they will operate with the heart of custodians. This is the life of extravagant givers—people who go over and above in their generosity.

Until we see our resources as not belonging to us, but as an opportunity for stewardship, we will not be the custodians God expects us to be. You cannot decide the purpose for the resources you have been charged with; you discover and deploy it.

I remember a prayer Pastor Chris Ugoh of The Kings Assembly, Nigeria prays. In this prayer, he proclaims that people will give their resources, time, talents, relationships and comfort to bless us. God used the little boy's five loaves of bread and two fish to feed over 5,000 men, women and children (John 6:1-15). God used the widow at Zarephath to feed Prophet Elijah (1 Kings 17:7-16). God used your boss—or someone in your office—to give you your job. These people were custodians of the resources and opportunities in their care, and they fulfilled the purpose of the resources. You are a custodian, and the resources in your care are tools God can use to change the lives of the people around you. The Domino Effect stops when we hoard or bury the favor and blessing that has been extended to us.

section three:
Generosity and Me

***Feel free to post quotes and pictures using the tags #generouscity and @victorehiemere

chapter 8

THE BLESSING OF GENEROSITY

> *My brethren, surely the time has come for us to return to the Lord's plan. Among us there are children to be clothed, widows to be aided, and afflicted ones to be cared for. As you draw near to the poor, the Saviour will come nearer to you.*
> *(George C. Lorimer)*[14]

Throughout the Bible, Greek and Hebrew words translated as *'bless'* occur over 400 times. While there are over 100 books and verses of the Bible that begin with the word *'blessed'*, including the book of Psalms and the longest chapter of the Bible (Psalm 119), we are most accustomed to the eight found in Matthew 5. The sermon on the mount, popularly referred to as The Beatitudes, is a collection of eight attitudes that unlock eight blessings. Bishop TD Jakes calls them *Blessed Attitudes*, and my mom calls them *Be-Attitudes*. I believe

---

[14] Gilbert, J. H. (1895). *Dictionary of burning words of brilliant writers: A cyclopædia of quotations from the literature of all ages.* New York: W.B. Ketcham.

beatitudes are supreme, next-level blessings that are only accessible to those brave and obedient enough to walk in the prerequisite attitudes.

In Acts 20:35, we learn of a new beatitude—the ninth beatitude, of sorts—from Jesus. While it is not recorded in any of the four gospels—we don't have a record of every word and action by Jesus (John 21:25)—the spirit of the message of Jesus can easily be seen in the text. When I meet Apostle Paul, I am going to give him a fist bump for rescuing this lost beatitude from the hallways of extinction. The mere fact he is reminding his readers of this beatitude shows that it was not foreign to his audience.

> *In everything I did, I showed you that by this kind of hard work we must help the weak, remembering the words the Lord Jesus himself said: <u>'It is more blessed to give than to receive.'</u> (Acts 20:35, NIV)*

In this text, Jesus teaches that the blessings of generosity stretch beyond the borders of getting back because you gave (Luke 6:38). And while this is the only verse that quotes Jesus outside of the four gospels, it is easy to see that it represents a big part of His message, and God's heart.

> *Where is another God like you, who pardons the guilt of the remnant, overlooking the sins of his special people? You will not stay angry with your people forever, <u>because you delight in showing unfailing love.</u> (Micah 7:18, NLT)*

> *Whatever is good and perfect is a gift coming down to us from God our Father, who created all the lights in the heavens. He never changes or casts a shifting shadow.(James 1:17, NLT)*

> *For who makes you different from anyone else? What do you have that you did not receive? And if you did receive it, why do you boast as though you did not? (1 Corinthians 4:7, NIV)*

> *Your attitude must be like my own, for I, the Messiah, did not come to be served, but to serve, and to give my life as a ransom for many. (Matthew 20:28, TLB)*

God is a giver, and He wants us to follow His example by living generous lives.

THERE IS A BLESSING IN RECEIVING

My most prominent love language is receiving gifts—specific gifts. If you want to make me really happy, buy me what I asked for; exactly what I asked for. Don't get creative! Copy and paste what I send you to amazon.com, and pay for whatever pops up. Do not look for related items, or what you think might be better. I have done my research and have read all the relevant reviews. I have explored the competition and settled on a choice. Your role, in this process, is paying for what I have picked out. No questions asked. Just buy what I asked for, down to the model number. It's that simple. I am serious.

With that said, you can understand my relief when I noticed that Jesus didn't say there is no blessing in receiving. In fact, receiving gifts is a blessing. Receiving lunch from

Chick-Fil-A when you are hungry is a humongous blessing. Paying for my vacation to any beautiful island is a blessing I will take any day. I could guarantee that it will be a blessing if I received a Dodge Charger with a supercharged 707-HP 6.2L Hemi® SRT Hellcat V8 Engine (Do you see how specific that was?). We all like being on the receiving ends of hugs, smiles, and other forms of kindness and love. Without receiving, we don't enjoy the love and appreciation of each other.

To survive on earth, we are recipients of the blessings of air, water, land, and the animals and plants that thrive on and in them. God is the ultimate source of everything we have received, physically and spiritually.

All praise to God, the Father of our Lord Jesus Christ, who has blessed us with every spiritual blessing in the heavenly realms because we are united with Christ. (Ephesians 1:3, NLT)

Our spirits are buoyant and vibrant when we walk in the spiritual blessings we receive from God, the chiefest of which is the assurance of eternal life with Him through Jesus Christ (Romans 6:23). When we fall and need a lifeline, God's mercy is a gift. When we are sick and ailing, the stripes Jesus took on our behalf, and the healing it gives us, are a gift. When we are in need of material resources, God's provision is a gift. We enjoy life to the fullest when we are on the receiving end of great gifts from God and other people.

I wish I could stop this narrative here, but I would be doing you a great disservice. Following Adam's lead, our natural proclivity tends to corrupt what was designed to be a blessing, turning it into a curse. In our selfishness, we can make the blessing of receiving our motivation for egocentricity. When receiving becomes an end in itself, we limit the power and the fullness of God's blessing for us.

LESSONS FROM A DEAD SEA

At more than 0.25miles below sea level, the shore of the Dead Sea—or Sea of Salt—is the lowest land elevation on Earth. Noted for its hypersalinity, and researched for its health and remedial potential, this body of water is more intriguing than any other body of water I know.

My research took an interesting turn when I inquired about the reasons behind its nomenclature. The sea is *dead* because its hypersalinity prevents fish and other macroscopic aquatic animals, and plants, from living in it. It gets better. The hypersalinity is due mostly to the fact that it has only the Jordan River as its main tributary. With the prevailing low rainfall levels and evaporation, the salinity of this body of water stays at exceptionally high levels.

Let's put it this way, for some reasons, the Dead Sea is *dead* because it receives water from the Jordan River, but is not positioned to pour into any other water-bodies. It reminds me of the, now popular, story of the rich fool in Luke 12. This man was on the receiving end of an unprecedented harvest, and like the Dead Sea, he made the decision to increase his hoarding infrastructure. He lost his life in the process. Per that story, the question is: 'Your money or your life?' Hoarding reverses the blessing of receiving.

Breath in. Hold it. Hold it. Hold it. Keep holding it while you read. Soon the words on this page will begin to blur and fade as your life slowly slips away from you. Hoarding—holding onto tightly what should be given away—cuts you off from God's supply and blessing on your life. God doesn't bless closed fists. Your hands must remain as open as they were when you received from God. If your outlet is not proportional to your inlet, you're setting yourself up for a disconnection from the Source.

And he went on to say to them all, "Watch out and guard yourselves from every kind of greed; because your true life is not made up of the things you own, no matter how rich you may be." (Luke 12:15, GNT)

While the world lauds us for what we have received and kept to ourselves, God stands in honor of our posture to give. Receiving is not the highlight of God's heart for you. Whilst there is some blessing in receiving, it is not the highlight of God's heart for you. There is a purpose to everything you have received, pleasure or business—doing business for God. In this divine purpose is greater and exceeding blessing.

THERE IS MORE BLESSING IN RECEIVING

"More blessings come from giving than from receiving.". (Acts 20:35, CEV. Emphasis, mine)

Now to the fun part.

It's important to note that Jesus didn't say that you will *love* giving more than you *love* receiving. He didn't say it will be more *natural* to give that to receive. Neither did He say, it will be *easier* to give than receive.

Jesus was—and still is—smart and purposeful. He knew this theme was going to cut against our natural grain. It is not easy to convince a selfish being to willingly relinquish what they have. Try getting a child to give up their candy willingly. It an uphill task to teach generosity to a generation that has been taught the contorted truth that the blessing of prosperity is in receiving and keeping more, and so much more. Even if the Greek word translated as *blessed* is also translated as *happy*, Jesus knew this was not going to be an easy lesson to teach.

Yes, God wants us to enjoy the blessing of receiving, but He also wants us to enjoy the even better, greater blessing of giving.

> *The world of the generous gets larger and larger; the world of the stingy gets smaller and smaller. The one who blesses others is abundantly blessed; those who help others are helped. (Proverbs 11:24-25, MSG)*

WE ARE MORE LIKE GOD WHEN WE GIVE

One of the days, while in the company of my friends, I asked Joel to pass along something one of my friends asked me for. Joel skipped over to me, took what I gave him, and hopped over to where my friend was sitting. A smile spread across

Joel's handsome face as my friend received the pack. Joel was evidently excited, and his joy overflowed when my friend thanked him for the gesture. He carried his head high like he had conquered an army. Then, my friend lifted up his face from my boy and expressed his gratitude to me. I wasn't expecting it; I was distracted by the other kids playing in the room. Joel drew my attention to my friend's gratitude, and I acknowledged it. Joel also ensured I said 'You're welcome.'

Here is the moral of the story. Just like Joel's obedience blessed my friend and consequently pointed the latter to me, our obedience blesses those who receive and, most importantly, points them to God, their Creator who loves them very much! In those 30 seconds, Joel was my extension. He did what I wanted, how I wanted when I wanted. He was me to my friend. Even though his little hands gave the gifts, they ultimately came from me. Do you get it?

We are extensions of God on the earth. People make their impressions of God from the way we live our lives. Our neighbors get their first taste of God from their interactions with us. It is our responsibility to ensure that this taste or impression is the right one. Stingy people cannot rightfully represent a generous God. Hoarders cannot represent a God, who gave His all and best.

As I wrote the preceding sentence, Jonathan MacReynolds's *Christ Representers* boomed through my headphones. Here are some of the lyrics.

We are Christ representers!

We are Christ representers!
And we shine our light so bright that we make them say Whoa
We gotta let them know that we are Christ representers
I've been anointed to be the light
It's in the way we walk; it's in the way we talk
It's in the way we live; it's in the way we give
It's in the way we praise, Jesus everyday
That we shine our light so bright that we make 'em say
Whoaa![15]

The way we give should make the world say Whoa! Before people step into a church building, we must have established the truth that the God we worship is the most generous being there is. We represent a God who doesn't just love; He is love!

When we give, we are extensions of God to those who receive God's blessings through us. God is a generous God, and when we are generous, we are most like Him. A greater blessing is reserved for people who are most like God—people who push past the elementary blessing of receiving, and press for the higher blessing of generosity.

GENEROSITY RESCUES US FROM SELFISHNESS

> *Don't look out only for your own interests, but take an interest in others, too. (Philippians 2:4, NLT)*

---

[15] Jonathan McReynolds (2015). Christ Representers. On Life Music: Stage Two [CD]. Entertainment One.

Earlier on, we established that in keeping with our natural propensity for selfishness, we are very likely to let the blessing of receiving hold us back from the greater blessing of generosity; turning a good thing into a curse. Breathing in is good for you only when you complete the cycle by breathing out. Break this natural cycle and you cut off your life supply. The natural cycle is receiving and giving, and receiving and giving. When we choke this blessing cycle with our selfishness and insistence on ourselves, we inadvertently cut ourselves from the richness of God's blessing to us.

> *Our world is drowning in a sea of self-centeredness. You can make yourself quite unique right away by leaving this ocean of selfishness and choosing to be curious about other people. (John Bytheway)[16]*

Selfishness produces a burden of responsibility. When we withhold what should be given, we despise the trust God has placed in us by blessing us. In doing so, we take on the responsibility for the security of our resources. We lose God's blessing over our resource when we take on the responsibility to protect and secure it.

> *Unless the Lord builds the house, those who build it labor in vain. Unless the Lord guards the city, the guard keeps watch in vain. (Psalm 127:1, NRSV)*

Selfish people are like dead pixels on a TV. Dead pixels are

---

[16] via www.brainyquote.com

pixels that have lost their light, and just appear as black spots on your screen They mess with the whole experience. Selfish people destroy what should be a beautiful expression of God's love and generosity.

When we are selfish, we experience *dead spots* in our spiritual lives. My house is a three-level house, and our wifi router doesn't quite cover the entire house. Movies freeze, downloads slow down to snail speed, and video chats cut off when we approach dead spots. Selfishness cut you off from the God's coverage. Selfishness blocks out God's voice and direction. Selfish hearts and minds do not interact very well with a sacrificial and generous God.

Generosity is the antidote to selfishness. Generosity uproots ego. Generosity refocuses our attention and energy where it is best served—blessing people with what we have been blessed with. When we are generous, we never see ourselves as the source of our resource. Generosity keeps us humble and usable by God.

> *This is how we've come to understand and experience love: Christ sacrificed his life for us. This is why <u>we ought to live sacrificially for our fellow believers, and not just be out for ourselves.</u> If you see some brother or sister in need and have the means to do something about it but turn a cold shoulder and do nothing, what happens to God's love? It disappears. And you made it disappear. (1 John 3:16-17, MSG)*

GENEROSITY POSITIONS ME TO RECIEVE MORE FROM GOD

By now, you have grasped that God watches our interaction and faithfulness with what we have now before He releases more to us. As custodians of the resources we have been blessed with, our most invaluable trait must be faithfulness. We trade in faithfulness. If God can trust it through you, He can trust it to you! Our generosity provokes God's generosity.

> <u>When you help the poor you are lending to the Lord</u>—and he pays wonderful interest on your loan! (Proverbs 19:17, TLB)

God doesn't owe any man any debts. When we help those in need, we activate God's help in our times and points of need. Your response to the needs around you determines God's response to your needs. Blessing others positions you to receive more blessings from God.

GENEROSITY ATTRACTS BLESSINGS FROM OTHERS

'Thank you.' Those are some of the most powerful words in the English language. It conveys appreciation from the blessed to the *blesser*. It connects the hearts of two people in ways second only to the words *'I love you'*.

Recently, I took my friend out for lunch. After we had enjoyed great Jamaican cuisine, he said, *"Thank you, bro. God bless you."* For some reason, those words resonated as they had never had before. I paid less than $40 for our lunch, and in return I was receiving blessings from God. What was $40 compared to the manifold supreme blessings of God? I was better off than when we left for lunch!

> *He will listen to the prayers of the destitute. He will not reject their pleas (Psalm 102:17, NLT)*

I think that some of the most powerful prayers are prayed by the people we bless. I can attest to that. One of the most powerful prayers I received came after I blessed one of my friends with a pair of shoes. His prayer extended to my destiny, and the fulfillment of God's work in and through me. If I had kept my money, and not bought those shoes, I would not have been blessed with that prayer. God hears the prayers of those we bless. And He answers them

Some of the greater blessings you will receive will be as a result of prayers made by people who cannot repay you in kind for your generosity.

> *<u>Those who give to the poor will lack nothing</u>, but those who close their eyes to them receive many curses. (Proverbs 28:27)*

GENEROSITY GRANTS ME ETERNITY WITH GOD

Nobody teaches this portion of scripture like my friend and pastor, Jimmy Rollins. He bases his conversation on Matthew 25.

> *"But when the Son of Man comes in his glory, and all the angels with him, then he will sit upon his glorious throne. All the nations will be gathered in his presence, and he will separate the*

people as a shepherd separates the sheep from the goats. He will place the sheep at his right hand and the goats at his left.

"Then the King will say to those on his right, 'Come, you who are blessed by my Father, inherit the Kingdom prepared for you from the creation of the world. For I was hungry, and you fed me. I was thirsty, and you gave me a drink. I was a stranger, and you invited me into your home. I was naked, and you gave me clothing. I was sick, and you cared for me. I was in prison, and you visited me.'

"Then these righteous ones will reply, 'Lord, when did we ever see you hungry and feed you? Or thirsty and give you something to drink? Or a stranger and show you hospitality? Or naked and give you clothing? When did we ever see you sick or in prison and visit you?'

"And the King will say, 'I tell you the truth, when you did it to one of the least of these my brothers and sisters, you were doing it to me!'

"Then the King will turn to those on the left and say, 'Away with you, you cursed ones, into the eternal fire prepared for the devil and his demons. For I was hungry, and you didn't feed me. I was thirsty, and you didn't give me a drink. "And he will answer, 'I tell you the truth, when you refused to help the least of these my brothers and sisters, you were refusing to help me.'

"And they will go away into eternal punishment, but the righteous will go into eternal life." (Matthew 25:31-42, 45-46, NLT)

In the end of our lives on earth, when we stand before God, we will be sorted by our interaction with the needs around us. Spiritual maturity is not complete without generosity. Apostle Paul says speaking in tongues is only noise if we don't live lives compelled and inspired by love (1 Corinthians 13:1).

It is more blessed to feed the hungry than it is to eat our favorite foods. It is more blessed to give away a cup of water than it is to drink water on a hot summer day. It is more blessed to invite people into your home than to go to your favorite celebrity's home. It is more blessed to cover other people's nakedness than it is to wear clothes by our favorite designers. It is more blessed to visit sick people in hospitals than to be visited when you are sick. It is more blessed to visit inmates in jail than it is to enjoy the company of your friends. It is more blessed to give than to receive! In doing this—in being generous—we secure eternal life connected to our loving Father.

chapter 9

THE OBEDIENCE OF GENEROSITY

What is more pleasing to the Lord: your burnt offerings and sacrifices or your obedience to his voice? Listen! Obedience is better than sacrifice… [17]

I am a second-generation pastor and preacher. My parents are some of the most articulate and impactful teachers of God's word I know. Growing up, I received on-going homiletic and hermeneutic training. I was raised in a church that started as a great Bible school, pastored by Dr. Emma and Chinyere Emma-Okorie, who prioritize sound and correct Biblical understanding.

During one of our impromptu sessions, as my dad gave me feedback on the first real sermon he heard me preach, he taught me what he called *foundation Scriptures*. Foundation

---

[17] 1 Samuel 15:22, NLT

Scriptures are Bible verses that form the foundation of a theological theme or topic. If you were to teach properly on a theme, you had to touch on the foundation scripture(s). For example, you couldn't sufficiently and rightly teach on Jesus' sacrifice for our sins and our subsequent salvation without touching John 3:16, Romans 10:9-10 and 1 John 1:9. They are considered foundational scriptures on the theology of salvation.

I have held onto one of the foundational Scriptures on giving and generosity until now. You can't talk about generosity without mentioning Luke 6:38.

<u>For if you give, you will get!</u> Your gift will return to you in full and overflowing measure, pressed down, shaken together to make room for more, and running over. Whatever measure you use to give—large or small—will be used to measure what is given back to you. (Luke 6:38, TLB)

I like the way The Message renders it. It touches on the reason I held onto this verse this long.

Give away your life; you'll find life given back, but not merely given back—given back with bonus and blessing. <u>Giving, not getting, is the way. Generosity begets generosity.</u> (Luke 6:38, MSG)

It is very easy to miss the point of Luke 6:38 because it is easy to focus on getting back for whatever we give that it slowly and surely becomes our motivation for giving. We live in very selfish times amongst a self-seeking and self-serving people.

Tell me I get $100 back for *giving* $1 and I will bend over backwards to *give* $1,000 because I want $100,000. And thus, we miss the point and God's heart for us.

Until you understand that your generosity is a part of God's global agenda and desire to reach the lost, least and last, you will go about it with the wrong motivation. Our motivation for living generously must be a desire to pass on the gifts and graces we have received from God to other people. Generosity is more than giving away food, water, sweaters or donating to a charity organization. It is meeting the needs of others from what you have been blessed with by God, and most importantly, in doing so, pointing them to God who becomes their source. True generosity turns people to God, not you. If people look to you instead of God, you have failed at being truly generous.

IT STARTS WITH A COMMAND

To truly capture it's true heart, we must recognize that Luke 6:38 begins with a command, *"Give..."*. We cannot breeze through the command and focus on the dependent consequence of the command. We cannot claim blessings, and refuse to operate in the context or premise of the blessings. They are not independent of each other. God is an *if-you-will-I-will* God. And by this, I don't mean we earn His love by doing things. I mean, God responds to our interaction with His commands. He wraps up His goodness in His commands and instructions.

When we stop to consider that this is like every other command, we draw closer to the true intent of this verse. And like every command from God, it demands obedience on our part. It is obedience to the command that releases the dependent consequence. For example, in Ephesians 6:1-2, we are commanded to obey and honor our parents. This obedience releases the blessing of long life. To access God's best for you, you must be willing to walk through the door of obedience. God has a soft spot for obedience.

One of the days Jesus was preaching and…

As he was speaking, a woman in the crowd called out, "God bless your mother—the womb from which you came, and the breasts that nursed you!"

Jesus replied, "But even <u>more blessed are all who hear the word of God and put it into practice.</u>" - (Luke 11:27-28, NLT)

If you are willing and obedient, you shall eat the best of the land… (Isaiah 1:19, AMP)

Obedience attracts God's attention. God rewards obedience. We show our love for God by our obedience. Our obedience to God invites us into a deeper relationship with Him.

If you love me, you will keep my commandments. (John 14:15, NRSV)

The person who has My commandments and keeps them is the one who (really) loves Me; and whoever (really) loves Me will

> *be loved by My Father, and I will love him and reveal Myself to him (I will make Myself real to him)."*
>
> *Jesus answered, "If anyone (really) loves Me, he will keep My word (teaching); and My Father will love him, and We will come to him and make Our dwelling place with him. (John 14:21, 23, AMP)*

Abraham would not have accessed the immense blessings God had for him if he had not obeyed the command to leave his fathers house (Genesis 12). If Noah hadn't obeyed the command to build the ark, he would have perished with the rest of the population of the world (Genesis 6-9). If Naaman had not obeyed the prophet and dipped seven times in the river, he would not have been healed of the disease (2 Kings 5). If the children of Israel hadn't followed God's instruction for the battle of Jericho, the wall would not have fallen (Joshua 6). God responds to obedience. It causes Him to release uncontainable favor on the obedient.

THE TEST OF OBEDIENCE

The charge to live generously is a test. It is a test that exposes the core motivations of our hearts. Matthew 6:21 teaches that our hearts reside in our treasures. If we treasure the gifts over the Giver of the gifts, we tend to hoard and withhold the gift. If we treasure the Giver over the gift, we are attentive to listen to His heart for the purpose of the gift.

Like every other form of obedience to God's command, we

don't decide how and when we obey the call to be generous. We obey how God instructs us when He instructs us and with what He instructs us.

I can't remember where I heard this story, but I will share it anyway. A pastor told a story of how God had prompted him to give one of his many suits to another pastor who wasn't doing as well as he was. Before I continue, it's important we understand that the Bible isn't the summation of God's word or heart for us. As concerns God's word, we have the written word of God—the Bible—and the spoken word of God. While the Bible has a lot of spoken words by God, God still speaks today. And as concerns generosity, God speaks everyday.

If you are honest, God had nudged you to give something away at some point in your life. Generally, this is how it works. You become sensitized to a need; you notice it wherever it may be found. And then it becomes a burden in your heart; a burden so big, you want to do something about it. This burden—the nudge to live beyond yourself—is God sharing His heart with you. Sometimes, this burden moves you to give to someone who is better off than you in most regards. It's still generosity. I dare say that generosity is more about obeying God than it is about the financial, physical or social condition of the recipient. You never know what God is going to do in them—and in you—through your generosity.

Back to my story. This pastor (let's call him Ed) hears God about giving away a suit, but there was one big problem. The suit he felt led to give away was the one he loved the most. It wasn't the most expensive; it was just *that* suit. It fit just right! Ed had a brilliant idea he thought was better than the nudge he had. He went into his closet, pulled out one of his more expensive suits and gave it to his pastor-friend. Amidst all the gratitude, Ed couldn't shake the burden. There wasn't a release yet. He asked his friend to wait, rushed to back to his closet and came back with five more suits. By now, his friend was almost on his knees, tears running down his face, filled with immense gratitude. But Ed still didn't feel a release. After one more trip to his closet, and bringing back a couple of suits that didn't include the one he *knew* he was to give, he finally gave in and obeyed what he *knew* he was supposed to do. And then the burden was lifted. By the end of this exercise, Ed had given out about 10 suits trying to give out one.

I believe that, to God, Ed gave out just one suit—the one he was supposed to. The other nine didn't count for obedience. Sometimes, we get lost in the sacrifice generosity entails that we lose sight of the obedience required. Sometimes, in our brilliance, we do what we think is right, abandoning what God says to do. Sometimes, God requires some specificity from us. I am reminded of how King Saul lost his leadership over Israel.

In 1 Samuel 15:3, God commands King Saul to *"... completely destroy the entire Amalekite nation—men, women, children, babies, cattle, sheep, goats, camels, and donkeys."* (NLT). But Saul had a *better* idea. He killed everyone except the king. He wanted to make a show of him as a warning to other enemy nations. He also *"... spared the best of the sheep, goats, and cattle...* ". They were going to be a great sacrifice to God. You would think God would have been pleased with this brilliant initiative. But no, God despised it! It was disobedience—it was like the sin of witchcraft (1 Samuel 15:23)

> *But Samuel replied, "What is more pleasing to the Lord: your burnt offerings and sacrifices or your obedience to his voice? Listen! Obedience is better than sacrifice, and submission is better than offering the fat of rams. (1 Samuel 15:22, NLT)*

God will always prefer obedience to him over our mundane ideas—no matter how great we think they are. Sometimes obedience will require a lesser quantity than what we want to sacrifice, and other times not. It's not about the amount than it is about obeying God. And when God doesn't give specific instructions, we can always fall back on what is already written or has been said in the past.

Living generously, like every other command, is blessed, primarily, because of obedience. When we engage the principle of generosity—obeying God's command to do so—we trigger the blessings of generosity.

YOUR OBEDIENCE IS THE SEED

In the Bible, giving is likened to sowing seeds. As custodians of the resources we have been blessed with, we are farmers. We sow seeds into people and trust God to grow His love, grace and transformation in them. Our generosity—the seeds we sow into people—produces a harvest of life change!

The farmer-seed-sowing parallel compares releasing your resources to others to putting seeds in the ground. And just as a harvest is a direct consequence of sowing, *getting* is a direct consequence of obeying the command to *give*. When we engage the principle of sowing, we get a bountiful harvest. They go hand in hand.

> *"While the earth remains, <u>seedtime and harvest</u>… shall not cease." (Genesis 8:22, AMP)*

And according to fundamental agricultural principles, the quality and quantity of your harvest are predicated, to a large extent, on the quality and quantity of your seed—your obedience, not necessarily the amount. Sow generously, and you will reap a generous harvest. Obey a few times—with hesitant regard and a stingy disposition—and you will reap a scanty harvest.

> *Remember this—a farmer who plants only a few seeds will get a small crop. <u>But the one who plants generously will get a generous crop.</u> (2 Corinthians 9:6, NLT)*

Recently, I had to reseed my lawn. In past summers, my lawn has not looked like the envy of the neighborhood I want it to be. So this year, I have gone all out. I did a soil test, checked my soil pH and N-P-K values, and corrected my abysmal Nitrogen levels (That's some pro stuff right there!). I tilled the bare spots, fertilized, and planted more seed than I believe I should have. Then, I covered the seed with some high-quality, pre-fertilized lawn soil. I am leaving nothing to chance! I have watered my lawn judiciously everyday since. This year has to be different. More seeds mean more grass. And more grass means an enviable lawn. That's the plan. That's what the internet reviews and commentaries claim should happen.

I believe that we have approached giving with the same mindset as I had to reseeding my lawn. And this mindset—of giving more to get more—has made us contort the truth of seed-sowing. We have turned giving and generosity into a financial scheme to get more blessings from God. While I don't have any problems with it, most people go as far as giving to charities just because they want more tax returns. Tax returns and multiplied blessings cannot be our motivation for generosity if we are to be true representations of God on earth. Our driving force must be obedience to God.

Our obedience is the seed. To the recipient of your generosity, that bottle of water or warm coat is a seed, but to you, your obedience is your seed. God uses the water and coat to work in their lives while He uses your obedience to work in and through your life. Do you get the picture? Our obedience to live generously affirms that we are willing participants in God's global mission to reach the world with His saving grace and mercy. If we don't obey the command to be generous, we cannot convince the world that God is generous.

Here's another way to put it: You're here to be light, bringing out the God-colors in the world. God is not a secret to be kept. We're going public with this, as public as a city on a hill. If I make

9: The Obedience Of Generosity

you light-bearers, you don't think I'm going to hide you under a bucket, do you? I'm putting you on a light stand. Now that I've put you there on a hilltop, on a light stand—shine<u>! Keep open house; be generous with your lives. By opening up to others, you'll prompt people to open up with God, this generous Father in heaven.</u> (Matthew 5:14-16, MSG)

Over the years, I believe we have focused on the seeds we are sowing rather than our obedience to God's command. When our focus is on what seed we are sowing, we are driven to *do more*—to sow more—because we want to receive more. When our focus is on obeying what God instructs—the burden He places on our hearts—our focus is to *do exactly*. *Doing exactly* is the true definition of obedience.

When we *do more*, we are motivated by a reward system. When we engage a reward system, the harvest becomes our treasure, and we leave ourselves vulnerable to manipulations that promise us more return if we sow more. In this contortion of the truth, we leave ourselves vulnerable to the deception that we work for what we have received, and therefore reserve the right to interact with it as we please. This can only go downhill (ask the rich fool in Luke 12).

When we *do exactly*, we are attentive to what God wants us to do because we understand our harvest is locked in the specificity of the seed He wants us to sow. When we *do exactly*, the harvest—what we get back—is not the focus; our obedience is. Our obedience triggers our harvest. When we *do exactly*, we are willing to die to ourselves—killing our selfish ambitions and pride—and submit ourselves to the will and purposes of God. Nobody said *doing exactly*—obeying—is always easy. But most assuredly, obeying God is the most rewarding endeavor you will undertake in.

Obedience might mean not buying that pair of shoes just yet, or ever. It might mean no summer vacations this year. Obedience might mean moving into a smaller house or the inconvenience of housing a young couple for a period of time. Whatever the obedience of generosity will require from you, it will produce a harvest of impact and life change in the benefactors of your obedience and a rich harvest in your life, no matter how painful it might seem when you are obeying. I like how the New Living Translation puts it.

> *I tell you the truth, unless a kernel of wheat is planted in the soil and dies, it remains alone. But its death will produce many new kernels—<u>a plentiful harvest of new lives</u>. (John 12:24, NLT.)*

> *Be generous: Invest in acts of charity. <u>Charity yields high returns.</u> (Ecclesiastes 11:1, MSG)*

A WIDOW, HER SON AND THEIR LAST MEAL

I couldn't end this chapter without talking about a widow, who unlocked an unlimited supply in her family through her obedience to a command to be generous,.

After Elijah had delivered God's instruction to King Ahab in 1 Kings 17 (God majorly spoke to His people through prophets in those times), God instructed the prophet Elijah to hide by a brook. He drank from the brook, and received meals from ravens! How cool is that? An animal that is notorious for preying on humans was the delivery agent of God's provision. God shows off like the sometimes. Nothing is impossible with Him.

Somehow in the midst of Elijah's obedience, the brook dried up. Bur God already had a plan in place. The difference with this plan was that it was predicated on the obedience of a widow in Zarephath. We pick up the story here.

> *Then the Lord said to Elijah, "Go and live in the village of Zarephath, near the city of Sidon. <u>I have instructed a widow there to feed you</u>."*
>
> *So he went to Zarephath. As he arrived at the gates of the village, he saw a widow gathering sticks, and he asked her, "Would you please bring me a little water in a cup?" As she was going to get it, he called to her, "Bring me a bite of bread, too."*
>
> *But she said, "I swear by the Lord your God that I don't have a single piece of bread in the house. And I have only a handful of flour left in the jar and a little cooking oil in the bottom of the jug. I was just gathering a few sticks to cook this last meal, and then my son and I will die." (1 Kings 17:8-12, NLT)*

Earlier on I said that sometimes our obedience might mean giving to someone who is better off than we are in some regards. This widow must have shared this sentiment. God was asking her to feed a prophet. In those days, Prophets were known for two things: hearing a word from God, and doing the miraculous.

Hours ago, ravens were feeding this prophet, and now he was asking for her last meal. Couldn't he find his next meal by some other (miraculous) means? Even though God had instructed her before the Prophet arrived in town (1 Kings 17:8-9), obedience seemed impossible, and irrational at best. It did not make sense to give away her last meal to a stranger—prophet or not. She had heard from God, but her struggle to obey was visible.

Elijah needed a meal, and this widow needed the security of more meals than the one she was about to prepare. Her last meal was an answer to the Elijah's prayer, but his hunger was the answer to her prayers. The ravens could have continued feeding Elijah, and all would have been well with him. But God wanted to do something in this widow's life. She had a need that God wanted to meet. God was going to meet her need based on her interaction with Elijah's need. Your generosity is God's way of meeting other people's need, but it has the power to produce a harvest that meets your needs.

Sometimes, God will put a need around you to meet a need in you. Sometimes, God will provide you with an opportunity and burden to give away some food—seed—because He wants to give you a harvest of physical healing. Your obedience with the seed—generosity—unlocks the harvest.

God provides for us based on our posture and interaction with the resources He blesses us with and the needs around us.

> *The rain and snow come down from the heavens and stay on the ground to water the earth. They cause the grain to grow, producing <u>seed for the farmer and bread for the hungry</u>. (Isaiah 55:10, NLT)*

> *For God is the one who provides seed for the farmer and then bread to eat. In the same way, he will provide and increase your resources and then produce a great harvest of generosity in you. (2 Corinthians 9:10, NLT)*

There is a sure harvest of generosity. This harvest is triggered by our posture of obedience and our interaction with our resources: *sowers* or *eaters*.

For the *eaters*—people who use their resources for themselves alone—God provides just enough. For the *sowers*—the generous people—God provides more than enough. It is critical to understand that seed sowers never lack food. They have food for years because God provides for others through them.

The widow at Zarephath was faced with two choices: be an *eater* with just a enough bread for one last meal, or be a *sower*, trust and obey God, and trigger a bountiful harvest of assured meals. What she had was barely enough for bread, but it was more than enough for seed.

> *But Elijah said to her, "Don't be afraid! Go ahead and do just what you've said, but make a little bread for me first. Then use what's left to prepare a meal for yourself and your son.*

For this is what the Lord, the God of Israel, says: There will always be flour and olive oil left in your containers until the time when the Lord sends rain and the crops grow again!"

<u>So she did as Elijah said</u>, and she and Elijah and her family continued to eat for many days. <u>There was always enough flour and olive oil left in the containers, just as the Lord had promised through Elijah.</u> (1 Kings 17:13-16, NLT)

This widow's sensitivity and obedience to God's instruction and burden on her heart turned barely enough food to more than enough food. It was not about the little bread she made for Elijah; it was about her willingness to obey God's instruction. Evidently, God could have fed Elijah by any other means. But this was designed to test and reward her obedience to release what she had for what God wanted her to have. Your next season of abundance might be locked up in your sensitivity and obedience to God's burden of generosity.

When we obey, we unleash the forest in our seed. When we obey, we multiply one life stirred and touched by God to many lives stirred and touched by God. The seed—bread—is a good blessing. It feeds you now. But the harvest is a richer, better blessing that secures your future.

<u>Give freely and become more wealthy</u>; be stingy and lose everything. <u>The generous will prosper</u>; those who refresh others will themselves be refreshed. (Proverbs 11:24-25, NLT)

QUICK THOUGHTS ON HARVESTS

Let me iterate that the pursuit of harvests cannot be our motivation for generosity. Generosity must flow from a heart committed to obeying God and representing him in the midst of the people and needs He has placed around us.

First, harvests are not always instantaneous. Sometimes they take time. My Friend, Steve, agreeing with a burden on his wife's heart, gave $500 to a need we had in church. They believed God for a successful sale of their house. In less than 24 hours after they posted their house, they received a bid from serious buyers. That was unprecedented! But their obedience released a quick harvest. They close on the house today. Sometimes that happens, and other times, it takes more time.

As I write these words, no blade of grass has appeared from the thousands of seeds I sowed in my lawn, but that doesn't stop me from watering my lawn every day. During our wait times, we must stay connected to the One we obeyed. God never forsakes His own. He is faithful to bring to pass what He has promised. Don't abandon your seed before it germinates. Water it with faith and trust in an unfailing God. Your harvest will surely come.

> *Once I was young, and now I am old. Yet I have never seen the godly abandoned or their children begging for bread. (Psalm 37:25, NLT)*

Second, harvests are not always obvious. You might not receive money for money. You will not always receive food for food. You might receive healing for giving out warm coats, or academic and business success for paying someone's bills. If our harvest is God's way of meeting our needs, we must trust that He knows what we need more than we do.

Miss Faye Johnson, a member of my church, during her first year with us, assisted us with obtaining a warehouse for our annual Christmas outreach initiative. We were in dire need of a great space to hold and distribute thousands of toy to less served kids in our community. Through her sensitivity and obedience, she made it happen. I don't think Miss Faye ever received a warehouse as her harvest. But I know where she received her harvest.

Months after she helped us with the warehouse space, she was diagnosed with cancer and given months to live. There have been ups and downs in her health. Some weeks have felt like her last. And in other weeks, you wouldn't guess she was sick. Now, over one year after she was given months to live, Faye is alive and getting stronger by the day. Guess where her harvest was? Yes! She is alive, against medical predictions, because she obeyed and responded to the need around her. She met the need for the warehouse and God met her need for healing even before she fell ill! Every need you are sensitized to is an opportunity to meet a need you might not even be aware of.

> *...for your Father knows exactly what you need even before you ask him! (Matthew 6:8, NLT)*

chapter 10

LIES ABOUT GENEROSITY

And you will know the truth, and the truth will set you free.[18]

The truth is powerful. The truth is not an opinion. The truth is not relative. The truth, that is, Jesus Christ, is the most powerful force on earth, and in heaven (John 14:6). We learn about the truth by paying attention to the words of Jesus and other God-inspired words.

The truth is our key to freedom. It breaks us out from the curse of the enemy's lies. A curse is a limitation. It is like a glass ceiling that lets you see what you can't have. The devil will tell you just enough lies to keep you from reaching for your best in God. The lies of the devil will keep you settled for a life below the mark God has pre-destined for you. The lies of the enemy will keep you from reaching out to a loving and forgiving

---

[18] John 8:32, NLT

Father.

Over the years, through personal experience and research, I have come to realize that whenever the devil wants to introduce a lie, he does one or more of the following:

- *Distorts the truth*
- *Strongly opposes the truth*
- *Minimizes the truth*
- *Exaggerates aspects of the truth*

The truth of generosity has suffered from all four of these attacks. People have believed a lie about the source of their resource. People have believed a lie about who owns what they hold. People have believed a lie that they can do whatever they please with their resources without consequences. People have believed a lie that everything that comes to them is for them.

Since this book is born out of a desire to share the truth about generosity, I thought it wise to deal with some lies the devil has told about generosity.

LIE #1: GENEROSITY IS ABOUT PROSPERITY

This truth has been attacked by lies that exaggerate aspects of what is true. God wants us to prosper. God desires that we have His best for us.

> *Let the Lord be magnified, <u>who delights and takes pleasure in the prosperity of His servant.</u> (Psalm 35:27, AMP)*

Remember, your Father knows exactly what you need even before you ask him! (Matthew 6:8, TLB)

Look at the lilies and how they grow. They don't work or make their clothing, yet Solomon in all his glory was not dressed as beautifully as they are.

And if God cares so wonderfully for flowers that are here today and thrown into the fire tomorrow, he will certainly care for you. Why do you have so little faith? (Luke 12:27-28, NLT)

God is not a wicked being high up in the skies who wants to lord it over you and your money. He genuinely wants what is best for you to come to you. God cares for you. He cares that you have bills that need to be paid. He cares that you need a new home, car or job. God cares for you.

When you consider all the Hebrew and Greek words that are translated as *prosperity* or *prosperous* in English Bibles, you begin to see God's heart for us.

- The Hebrew word *Tsalach* means *to push forward, to break forth, to be profitable, to make progress*
- The Hebrew word *Shalowm* means *completeness (in number), safety and soundness in body, welfare, health, peace (from war), quiet, contentment, tranquility*
- The Hebrew word *Shelev* means *ease*
- The Hebrew word *Towb* means *good, pleasant, agreeable, excellent, bounty, welfare*
- The Greek word *Euodoo* means *direct and easy way, speedy way, successful*

God wants to push you forward into better things. He wants

you to enjoy safe and sound life in the completeness of His blessings. God wants you to be successful. God wants you to prosper. And this prosperity is not just about money. It is about favor, acceleration, uncommon miracles and deliverances. This prosperity is the summation of the full life that God promises in John 10:10. This is the truth.

Even though God is a God of truth, He is also a God of principles. If you get and stay on Route 66, and head west, you will end up in Santa Monica, California, no matter how hard you pray and fast. Principles are like paths that lead to a predetermined destination. God honors principles. Look at how Luke 12 continues.

> <u>And don't be concerned about what to eat and what to drink.</u> Don't worry about such things. These things dominate the thoughts of unbelievers all over the world, but your Father already knows your needs. <u>Seek the Kingdom of God above all else, and he will give you everything you need.</u> (Luke 12:29-31, NLT)

Seek the kingdom of God (God's way of doing things) and the things that others worry about will come to you naturally. That's the principle. And God honors it. Your generosity plays a major part in God's strategy to spread and expand His kingdom on the earth. Seek out and engage in ways to expand the kingdom of God on earth, and God will *"...give you everything you need."*

But even though *getting* is a natural consequence of *giving*, it cannot be the motivation for giving. Obedience must be the motivation for generosity. Anything less will deny us from receiving the fullness of what God has for us. Generosity with an eye on what will be received in return is selfishness of the highest order.

The lie of the enemy causes us to exaggerate aspects of the message of prosperity that focuses us on giving to get, turning the message of Jesus into a financial gimmick. And when truth is exaggerated—and is now a lie—it makes promises it cannot fulfill. I have heard people recount tales of how they gave expecting to receive so and so and didn't receive anything. While there could be many reasons for this, I believe a good majority of the people gave, not out of obedience, but out of what they stood to get. That is selfish generosity, and selfish generosity does not honor or obey God. Selfish generosity is not true generosity.

Many people have a bitter taste in their mouths, disbelieving the truth that God wants the best for them. This lie has placed a lot of people under a curse. It has stopped people from living the generous life God requires of them.

God wants us to prosper, but He wants us to prosper in obedience to Him. Your obedience is more important than whatever prosperity you are seeking. And even though God wants you to prosper, that is just the beginning. God wants you to move from prosperity to generosity. God wants you to move from seeking for yourself to seeking out ways to bless other people. God wants us to desire resources to come through us than we desire resources to come to us. God wants us to move from selfish living to living beyond ourselves.

God is able to make it up to you by giving you everything you need and more <u>so that there will not only be enough for your own needs but plenty left over to give joyfully to others.</u>

It is as the Scriptures say: "The godly man gives generously to the poor. His good deeds will be an honor to him forever."

For God, who gives seed to the farmer to plant, and later on good crops to harvest and eat, will give you more and more seed to plant and will make it grow so that you can give away more and more fruit from your harvest.

Yes, God will give you much so that you can give away much, and when we take your gifts to those who need them they will break out into thanksgiving and praise to God for your help. (2 Corinthians 9:8-11, TLB)

When we allow ourselves to be stuck in prosperity with no generosity, we stunt our spiritual growth and sabotage our connection with the one true Source (Luke 12:16-20).

LIE #2: THE LESS YOU HAVE THE LESS ACCOUNTABLE YOU ARE

This is one big lie that we must be delivered from. Accountability is not dependent on quantity and volume. Accountability is accountability no matter who you are or what you have.

As Joel gets older, we have begun teaching him some relevant life lessons, especially regarding his interaction with other people. One of the many lessons he is learning is how to use words respectfully. Amby, my wife, and I taught him that on no occasion should he say *shut up* to anyone. There are nicer ways to communicate the sentiment.

One of the days, during a conversation, I told my friends to *shut up*, and Joel was in the room. You can imagine his reaction. He quickly turned to me and rebuked me, "*Daddy, we don't say that!*" Somewhere in my mind, I thought being an adult exempted me from the rules. But Joel was there to remind me that accountability is no respecter of persons. My age didn't exempt me from the rules.

In the story of the talents in Matthew 25, a man gives three varying amounts of money to his three servants. When it was time to give an account of how they managed the money, all three were held to the same standard. To the two servants who did what he asked, he said the same thing.

> *After a long time their master returned from his trip and called them to give an account of how they had used his money. The servant to whom he had entrusted the five bags of silver came forward with five more and said, 'Master, you gave me five bags of silver to invest, and I have earned five more.'*
>
> *The master was full of praise. 'Well done, my good and faithful servant. You have been faithful in handling this small amount, so now I will give you many more responsibilities. Let's celebrate together!'*

> *The servant who had received the two bags of silver came forward and said, 'Master, you gave me two bags of silver to invest, and I have earned two more.'*
>
> *The master said, 'Well done, my good and faithful servant. You have been faithful in handling this small amount, so now I will give you many more responsibilities. Let's celebrate together!'*
> *(Matthew 25:19-23, NLT)*

Even though the first servant came back with ten talents, six more than the servant with an initial two, both of them received the same response from their master. And when the third servant stepped up to give his account, the expectations were not lower because he had received just one talent. I believe the servant with the five talents would have received the same consequence as the servant with one talent if he had mismanaged the money he received.

You are held to the same level of accountability whether you are a five, two or one talent person. You should not be more generous because you have more. I dare say that generosity is not measured in actual amounts, but in percentages. If I give 10 out of 20, I am more generous than someone who give 20 out of 1,000. If I give 1 out of 20, I am less generous than someone who gives 500 out of 1,000 even if I have less.

> *Jesus sat down near the collection box in the Temple and watched as the crowds dropped in their money. Many rich people put in large amounts. Then a poor widow came and dropped in two small coins.*

Jesus called his disciples to him and said, "I tell you the truth, this poor widow has given more than all the others who are making contributions. For <u>they gave a tiny part of their surplus</u>, but she, poor as she is, has given <u>everything she had to live on</u>."
(Mark 12:41-44, NLT)

True generosity is sacrificial, and sometimes it can mean giving all we have. It costs to be generous. But we have the confident assurance that God pays attention to our obedience to sacrifice. And He rewards it.

The burden of generosity is not predicated on how much you make. Your heart to obey God's command compels you to live beyond yourself, no matter what your bank balance is. The Holy Spirit keeps the burden of generosity from being a weight that saddens or depresses us. True generosity frees you up to live in God's abundance.

LIE #3: IT DOESN'T MATTER HOW YOU GIVE

True generosity is not just about what you give, but how you give. How you give can qualify or disqualify what you give. Have you ever received something from someone only to leave their presence feeling less of a human than when you walked in? Generosity should leave the recipient feeling better and bigger than before you encountered them. Generosity is life giving; it should infuse the recipient with the life of God.

In 2 Corinthians 9, Apostle Paul is writing to a church about how exemplary and inspiring their generosity was to the other churches he was visiting. Since he was writing to a group of people who were generous, he didn't talk about what should be given. He deals with how they were to give.

> *That is why I thought it necessary to urge these brothers to go to you (before I come) and make arrangements in advance for this generous, previously promised gift of yours, so that it would be ready, not as something extorted (or wrung out of you), but as a (voluntary and) generous gift.*
>
> *Now (remember) this: he who sows sparingly will also reap sparingly, and he who sows generously (that blessings may come to others) will also reap generously (and be blessed). Let each one give (thoughtfully and with purpose) just as he has decided in his heart, not grudgingly or under compulsion, for <u>God loves a cheerful giver (and delights in the one whose heart is in his gift)</u>.*
> (2 Corinthians 9:5-7, AMP)

Generosity Should Be Planned

> *… make arrangements in advance for this generous, previously promised gift of yours, so that it would be ready…*

Anytime I hear someone has decided to get more financially intelligent and seek financial order, I usually ask to see what their budget looks like. I look for two things. Amidst the lines for bills, car notes and debts, I search for lines that represent generosity to God and generosity to other people. Where is the money set aside to buy a cup of coffee for that co-worker? Where is the money set aside to buy non-perishable food for the local food pantry? Where do you have Christmas shopping for the kids in the local orphanage? Where is generosity on your budget? Sometimes, we think that after bringing back out tithe (10%), we can do whatever we want with the rest. God still has a purpose for the 90%. Stay in tune with him to chart a generosity plan.

> *I want each of you to take plenty of time to think it over, and make up your own mind what you will give. (2 Corinthians 9:7, MSG)*

Until generosity is a line item on your budget, it will not be a burden on your heart. Sometimes you need to write it down on your budget before you feel like giving it. Planning to be generous preserves the integrity of generosity. If you don't plan to be generous, it will be the first thing you give up when things are tight. Anytime people walk up to me and express their need to stop tithing or giving for a period of time because of how tight things are, my logical mind understands, but my spirit is troubled because I can only imagine what they are locking themselves out of.

Another big lie of the enemy is that we are supposed to give from what is left. If you wait until you have paid your bills to give to God and others, you will find that you will rarely do it. The last on the list is usually the first off the list. The first thing you spend on when you get paid determines the direction the rest of your resources will go. Make your tithe—giving to God—the first, and watch Him bless the rest.

> *Now regarding your question about the money being collected for God's people in Jerusalem. You should follow the same*

procedure I gave to the churches in Galatia. On the first day of each week, you should each put aside a portion of the money you have earned. Don't wait until I get there and then try to collect it all at once. (1 Corinthians 16:1-2, NLT)

Generosity must be planned and intentional if it will remain a priority. When you receive any income, set aside what is going to be given away. Some part of everything that comes to you is designed to go through you.

Generosity Should Not Be Out of Compulsion

… so that it would be ready, not as something extorted (or wrung out of you)… not grudgingly or under compulsion…

The New Life Version says our giving should *"… be a true gift and not something you were made to do."* Pastor Jimmy Rollins put it this way, "Give out of revelation, not compulsion or obligation."

Even if obedience is the motivation for true generosity, we shouldn't do it because we are *supposed to*. We must give from a place of joy and dedication, not reluctance and obligation. We don't give because we have to give. We give because we get the privilege to. An opportunity to be generous is an expression of God's trust in you. He trusts that He can pass a blessing through you to others. This honor should not be approached lightly or taken for granted.

Generosity Should Be Generous

... but as a (voluntary and) <u>generous gift</u>. Now (remember) this: he who sows sparingly will also reap sparingly, <u>and he who sows generously (that blessings may come to others) will also reap generously (and be blessed)</u>...

Sounds redundant, I know. But if we are going to be generous, we have to be generous.

Giving sparingly means sowing with restraint. It means giving with an eye on what is left. I have a dear friend (whose name will remain unmentioned) who would rather lose a foot than share his pastries or desserts with you. He will rather point out where you can buy your cupcake so that he doesn't share his with you. One of the days, I asked for one of his five cupcakes, and you would think I asked for all five! He couldn't spare one out of five! His countenance fell as he hesitantly handed me the cake. He made sure to express how four cupcakes were not going to satisfy his cravings. He gave me with an eye on what was left. He gave with what was spared. He gave sparingly!

Generosity gives with an eye on the impact that it is making. Generosity gives with the consciousness that what is left still doesn't belong to us. Generosity gives to obey God's leading. Giving generously honors God, blesses others and blesses us.

Generosity Should Be Cheerful

…for God loves a <u>cheerful giver (and delights in the one whose heart is in his gift)</u>.

Some of us need to tell our faces that our hearts are in our giving. Like my *pastry-friend*, most of us give with a frown on our faces. Jesus didn't grumble all the way to his death on the cross. If you will not smile when you give, don't give at all.

The Greek word for cheerful is *hilaros*, and it means to be cheerful and joyous. It is from this word we get the English word *hilarious*. There is nothing sad, reluctant or gloomy about *hilaros*. Generosity without joy is not generosity; it is just forced giving, and God doesn't honor it.

Truly generous people love what they do. And they know their smile or their cheerful and caring disposition might work more miracles than the food or clothes they are giving away. Assume the position of the recipient, and you will learn the wonders a smile can work.

When we are generous, how we give holds as much importance as what we give.

LIE #4: GENEROSITY IS NOT SPIRITUAL

This lie has made us relegate the act of giving to a physical, mathematical act of crunching numbers. Nothing could be further from the truth. While generosity is not just about your money, your money plays a big part in it. Money is not just money. Money is your heart's currency. Your heart is captured by what it treasures (Luke 12:34). Your heart worships what it treasures.

Your money is spiritual. Your interaction with your money is spiritual. Money has a spirit that promises all that God promises: security, peace, and joy. But we know money doesn't deliver on the promises it makes. Ever heard the saying, 'More money, more problems.'? Only God delivers on His promise of security, peace, joy and abundance.

> *If the Lord does not build the house, it is useless for the builders to work on it. If the Lord does not protect a city, it is useless for the guard to stay alert. (Psalm 127:1, GW)*

Generosity is an Act of Worship

Generosity—especially to God—is an expression of worship to Him. All through the Bible, there are accounts of people who reinforced their words of worship with sacrifices. We worship God with our time, talents and treasures. We must have the same fervor to worship God with our money as we do with our time and skills. I know many people who will serve on every team in church, but shrink at the mere mention of money in church. With our resources, we must worship God, who gave His best and only for us.

Generosity Acknowledges and Honors Our Source

When we are obedient to God through our generosity, we

acknowledge that we are mere custodians of the resources we have received. As in the parable of the talents, God honors and rewards people whom He can trust His blessings through.

Generosity Is The Overflow of a Stirred Spirit

In Luke 19, Zacchaeus encounters Jesus, and his life is changed forever. Once a selfish, self-serving man, Zacchaeus decides to give away half of his wealth to the poor! His spirit was so stirred that he wanted everyone to experience what he had experienced. Generosity overflows from a spirit that is overcome by the love of Jesus. If you experience the grace God gives, you have no option than to show the same grace to others. If God has blessed you in a season of lack, you find yourself willing to give to people in their season of lack. True generosity is the result of a spiritual encounter, one stirred spirit stirring another spirit.

I discussed this in-depth in Chapter 3: Generosity Is Spiritual.

When we walk in the truth of generosity, we unlock blessings of generosity in our lives. And this truth will set you free to live in the abundance God desires for you.

chapter 11

GENEROSITY AS A MEMORIAL

"What I spent, is gone; what I kept, I lost; but what I gave away will be mine forever." (Ethel Percy Andrus)[19]

I recently stumbled on *In Loving Memory* by Alter Bridge, and I thought some of the words set the scene for what this chapter covers.

> *I carry the things that remind me of you*
> *In loving memory of*
> *The one that was so true*
> *You were as kind as you could be*
> *And even though you're gone*
> *You mean the world to me*[20]

---

[19] via www.izquotes.com
[20] Alter Bridge (2004). In Living Memory. On One Day Remains [CD]. Wind Up.

This song, released in 2004, could have been relevant over 2000 years ago when the true story of Dorcas played out.

IN LOVING MEMORY (DORCAS' STORY)

In Acts 9, we are brought in on what can be considered the most significant conversion in the New Testament. Saul, who later become Apostle Paul, encounters God on his way to persecute and kill Christians. His life is never the same again. He immediately begins to preach in Damascus.

Further down in the text, Peter is traveling from place to place, preaching the word of God and healing sick people. In Lydda, he heals a man who had been paralyzed and bedridden for eight years. In verses 1 through 35, we have a first-hand view of the ministries of two of the greatest apostles of all time, Peter, and Paul. And for some reason, when it would have been appropriate to talk about Apostles John, James, or any of the other disciples, we are introduced to Dorcas. She was an everyday Christian.

Dorcas is a woman who lived in Joppa. She did many kind things for others. She was not an apostle, but God thought her life was noteworthy enough to be featured alongside Peter and Paul. In the text, it is easy to see why this woman's story is important to God.

11: Generosity As A Memorial

In the city of Joppa there was a woman named Dorcas ("Gazelle"), a believer who was always doing kind things for others, especially for the poor.

About this time she became ill and died. Her friends prepared her for burial and laid her in an upstairs room. But when they learned that Peter was nearby at Lydda, they sent two men to beg him to return with them to Joppa.

This he did; as soon as he arrived, they took him upstairs where Dorcas lay. The room was filled with weeping widows who were showing one another the coats and other garments Dorcas had made for them.

But Peter asked them all to leave the room; then he knelt and prayed. Turning to the body he said, "Get up, Dorcas," and she opened her eyes! And when she saw Peter, she sat up! He gave her his hand and helped her up and called in the believers and widows, presenting her to them. (Acts 9:36-41, TLB)

In Matthew 25, we see that God pays attention and judges us based on our interaction with the needs around us. If we forsake and ignore the needs around us, we cut ourselves from eternity with Him. If we understand the import of Matthew 25, we see why God would let the story of an untitled Christian woman lie in the same context as that of two of the most spiritual personalities of Christianity.

Today, one of my colleagues at i5 CHURCH transitioned from being on staff. On her last day, we sat around the conference table, recounting how much of a blessing she had been. There were tears, sniffs, and laughter. Lavalle had touched our lives during her time on staff. From her smiling face to the music she played in her office, to her delicious queso dip, Lavalle was going to be missed dearly. What stood out the most was that this heart of kindness wasn't just apparent during her nine to five job. Lavelle and her husband, Milton, have been known to take in kids, train them and release them as responsible, contributing members of society. Lavalle was naturally generous. Long after she has transitioned, she will be remembered. I will go to work next Tuesday, and I will miss seeing her face as I make my way to my office.

GENEROSITY ACTIVATES GOD FOR YOU

Peter had just healed Aeneas from eight years of paralysis when two men burst into the room demanding and pleading that he went with them. Their friend was dead. As they journeyed down from Lydda to Joppa, the two men told Peter stories that proved this dead woman was very different from every other dead woman before her. For one, this was one woman who couldn't stay dead. She was, literally, too good to die.

When Peter arrived on the scene, he was met with physical manifestations of Dorcas' kindness. All around the room, widows displayed clothes and coats that Dorcas had made for them. This was their argument when they sought help for her.

This is the only time in the Bible when a person is raised from the dead because of their impact on the lives of others.

These widows didn't have the resources to make her a garment or pay her for what she had made for them. Nothing they could give her was relevant now since she was dead. They didn't have money, but they were persuaded she deserved to live. They were willing to do anything to see that happen.

The most powerful prayers you will ever receive will come from people who cannot repay you in kind for your generosity. Some of the most significant blessings you will receive will come from people you have been kind to. Psalm 102:17 says God listens to the prayer of the poor. When they make pleas to God or bless you, He listens. If God can activate you for others when they call upon Him, He will activate others to help you when you need it. If we spend our time on our knees in service to others, they will spend their time on their knees in prayer for us.

Oh, the joys of those who are kind to the poor! The Lord rescues them when they are in trouble.

The Lord protects them and keeps them alive. He gives them prosperity in the land and rescues them from their enemies.

The Lord nurses them when they are sick and restores them to health. (Psalm 41:1-3, NLT)

Those who shut their ears to the cries of the poor will be ignored in their own time of need. (Proverbs 21:13, NLT)

GENEROSITY LIVES BEYOND YOUR YEARS

What if you are remembered for as long, in years, as the number of people you were generous with? Many of our memories would not last past 20 years. Other than a good name, the best legacy anyone can have is a generous name.

> *It is as the Scriptures say: "The godly man gives generously to the poor. <u>His good deeds will be an honor to him forever.</u>" (2 Corinthians 9:9, TLB)*

There is a memorial building in Skopje, Macedonia, dedicated to humanitarian and Nobel Peace Prize laureate Mother Teresa[21]. Even though she passed in 1997, she will be remembered for founding Missionaries of Charity that runs HIV/AIDS, leprosy and tuberculosis hospices, soup kitchens, mobile clinics, orphanages, and schools. She dedicated her life to give *"wholehearted free service to the poorest of the poor."*[22] No matter the controversies that surrounded some of her actions and stands, she will forever be remembered for her exemplary generous living.

We will only be remembered for what we have done, not for all the big words we used. We will be remembered more for showing we love people than for saying we do. We will be remembered for feeding the hungry than for what food we ate when we were hungry. We will be remembered for the naked

---

[21] via en.wikipedia.org/wiki/Mother_Teresa
[22] Muggeridge (1971), chapter 3, "Mother Teresa Speaks", pp. 105, 113

people we clothed than for the clothes we wore. We will be remembered by what generous acts we have done.

During the funeral ceremony of C. H. Spurgeon, Ira D. Sankey set to music the words of Dr. Horatius Bonar in the hymn *Only Remembered*[23].

> *Only remembered, only remembered,*
> *Only remembered by what we have done;*
> *Thus, would we pass from the earth and its toiling,*
> *Only remembered by what we have done.*
>
> *Shall we be missed though by others succeed,*
> *Reaping the fields we in springtime have sown?*
> *No, for the sowers may pass from their labors,*
> *Only remembered by what they have done.*
>
> *Only the truth that in life we have spoken,*
> *Only the seed that on earth we have sown;*
> *These shall pass onward when we are forgotten,*
> *Fruits of the harvest and what we have done.*

Generosity preserves our names—and God's name—in the annals of time.

GENEROSITY TRIGGERS MORE THAN WE KNOW

Weeks after she joined our staff as the Outreach Director, Charity shared a unique story of how a bag of groceries

---

[23] Sankey, Ira David. My Life and the Story of the Gospel Hymns. Harper & Brothers, 1906.

changed a girl's life forever.

After pushing through what she thought was not enough in the first place, Charity, and her team, gave out bags of groceries to less-served people in her community. A month or so later, a young lady saw her and eagerly offered to share her story of restored hope.

This lady, at six years old, was prostituted by her mother to feed a drug addiction. This catapulted her on a downward spiral into depression, drug addiction, and homelessness. It was in this state that Charity met her, and gave her a bag of groceries. That bag of groceries inspired hope within this young lady. She was infused with so much hope, that she decided to break her drug addiction, go back to school, and do something with her life. One bag of groceries changed her life. Here is a quote from Charity's story.

It wasn't really about the groceries at all. I was the answer to her prayers. I was carrying a miracle. The bag of groceries infused her with hope. God uses people to bring hope, to bring mercy… to bring His grace to the people we meet. I believe that some of the people we meet on outreaches, will eventually lead outreaches one day.

If generosity is spiritual, it then means its impact is more than physical. The impact and effects of true generosity are spiritual. It inspires hope and has eternal consequences greater than we could ever comprehend. Our generosity turns people to our generous God. That's God's Domino Effect!

11: Generosity As A Memorial

He will always make you rich enough to be generous at all times, so that many will thank God for your gifts which they receive from us.

For this service you perform not only meets the needs of God's people, but also <u>produces an outpouring of gratitude to God.</u>

And because of the proof which this service of yours brings, <u>many will give glory to God</u> for your loyalty to the gospel of Christ, which you profess, and for your generosity in sharing with them and everyone else. (2 Corinthians 9:11-13, GNT. Emphasis, mine)

conclusion

THE CHARGE TO GENEROSITY

> *God can bless you with everything you need, and <u>you will always have more than enough to do all kinds of good things for others</u>.* [24]

Generosity occurs when one stirred spirit stirs another spirit. It is not so much about money as it is about reaching out, in obedience to others with what blessings you have received from God.

> *Command them to do good, to be rich in good works, to be generous and ready to share with others. (1 Timothy 6:18, GNT)*

For a long time, I wrestled with how best to end this book. I didn't want this experience to end like any other. I wanted it to

---

[24] 2 Corinthians 9:8, CEV

end as memorably as it could. In the midst of my search, I stumbled upon a speech that I wish I wrote myself.

Here is Gina Rodriguez's acceptance speech for receiving the Young Humanitarian Award at Variety's unite4:humanity benefit.

I grew up in the hood of Chicago. We didn't have much, but that didn't stop my parents from working the hardest they could to provide for three girls. And as if that was not enough, they went on to help everyone else.

My mom would cook for everybody in the neighborhood. On weekends, her and my father collected the kids to paint [over] graffiti and clean the streets.

I remember being about 13 years old; I would go with my dad to his negotiations. (He was a Teamster. Being a Teamster, he was like the protective elder brother of all the union workers he represented.) And I would watch him lay his own job on the line for somebody's equal rights. I would watch my mom sacrifice every luxury for us, for our extended family, for the person that came into her path, just to make sure they were happy and fulfilled. And they did this. They did this day in and day out.

They set the trend. They taught me that being good was a standard that doesn't need praise or recognition. That [as] you help others succeed, you too will succeed.

In a culture that we live in—[one] that praises people for doing good—this isn't a reward that I worked towards, unlike acting, unlike Jane The Virgin. This is me. This is my heart.

> *I love what-ifs. What if I book a show? What if I win a Golden Globe? Or what if we lived in a world where booking a show and getting a Golden Globe was just an excuse to do good for others? Confession—that's the world I'm trying to create. A place where Oscar winners eradicate homelessness. A place where Grammy winners help provide and contribute to curing cancer. A place where we all leverage our social currency to do something that truly matters. Adopt children that need homes, finance tuition for kids that don't have the money to go to college; the list goes on. It's a world where the true award is giving.*
>
> <u>*My heart was molded to fill fulfillment when I am [able] to help others.*</u> *Good is the food that I give my heart. Thank you, mom and dad, for teaching me this.*
>
> *To my siblings, who taught me that <u>you give graciously, or you don't give at all,</u> thank you for being the blueprint of that path for me.*
>
> *This award will be used for motivation that I never stop growing in character, that I never stop growing in being a source for others, and giving of my blessings. And most importantly, as a reminder <u>that the world I want to live in is one of service, one that the true award, again, is [in] giving</u>.*
>
> <u>*May I always seek that award [of giving] over every other.*</u> *So, thank you for tonight.*

Now that you know the truth, go and live beyond yourself! Go and impact your world! We are citizens of the Generous City, and we have been called to share our lives with the world.

Here is my charge to you and I implore you to read it aloud as often as you can.

I will go into the world and be extravagantly generous. I will feed the hungry, give water to the thirsty, welcome the homeless, clothe the naked, care for the sick and destitute, and visit the imprisoned.

I will give to people less served than I am. I will be generous even with those who seem better served than I am because it's the obedience that matters the most.

I understand that what I have is not mine. I am blessed to be a blessing. I am a custodian for God; fulfilling His purposes for what He has blessed me.

I will be sensitive to the needs around me because they are opportunities to unlock Gods manifold blessings over my life. I understand that my generosity is a seed, and I commit to sowing with every chance you get. As long as the earth remains, seedtime and harvest will not cease. I will surely reap a bountiful harvest for every seed I sow. Even though I will receive for giving, that must never be my motivation for giving. Obedience to God must be my driving force. I will give out of revelation and not compulsion.

Finally, my generosity is a vital part of God's strategy to draw people to His freeing power and saving grace. Some part of everything that comes to me is designed to go through me. If I live selfishly, I misrepresent my generous God and placate his Domino Effect.

God gave His best, His one and only for me. I must be willing to do the same for others.

I am a citizen of the Generous City.

acknowledgements

FIRST, THE SERIOUS ONES,

To my 'babe', who pushes me to become all God designed me to be. Thank you for making sure I don't settle in complacency. You mean the world to me. I will love you till I die.

To my son, Joel, thank you for going to bed on time, and leaving me hours to write this book. Daddy loves you!

To my dad and mom, who laid a solid spiritual foundation in me. Mom, your heart for the less served is still a massive challenge and inspiration to me!

To Pastor Jimmy Rollins, who commissioned me to write this book when he interrupted me mid-sermon. I will not forget that day, and will never take for granted the trust you have placed in me. Thanks, bro!

To Rhema, who told me to just write. I did just that. I wrote this book on my couch. Who knew I could? You did!

To Pastor Steve Harris, you told me to keep pressing, and not give up. Thanks for the words of encouragement and chastisement, when necessary.

To Irene Rollins, Sherrie Harris, Udeme Umuna, Larry Mack, Nkiru Ehiemere, and Nadine Green, who walked with me from the very beginning. Thank you for taking out time from your busy schedules to partner with me. This is for you.

To Kwanza Gipson, who sat with the reborn author I have become. I still owe you a book and this author is ready to deliver! Bring it on!

To the staff of i5 CHURCH, who have suffered through being my sounding board and laboratory. I love what we have become—a family!

To i5 CHURCH, what can I say?!? You are the best community anyone could ask for. You challenge me to be lead better, speak better, and most importantly, be better. We are a city that cannot be hidden!

To the reader, this one is for you. I believe God wants to activate you in ways you cannot comprehend. It's time to change the world!

NOW, FOR SOME HUMOR

To my Audio-Technica ATH-M50x, you isolated me from the noise and created a sound field like no other before you. Thanks to Wes for pointing me to these gems. They are better than my Bose and Beats. To Apple, my MacBook is a gift from God. Thank you for being excellent.

To the people behind BibleGateway.com, you rock! You made this easier. To William McDowell, your Sounds of Revival album is the soundtrack of this project. That was all I could listen to without being distracted. You did something right on that one. By the way, Will and I are friends!

To the team behind Ulysses, it truly is the *Ultimate App*

for Anyone Who Writes. To Miladinka Milic (Meela) from 99 Designs, thank you for accepting my invitation to join the design contest. See? You won! Thank you to the inventor of the HDVR, your work let me write at night and catch up with my shows during the day!

To Arsenal Football Club, our titleless run has built resilient hope in me. But for the sake of the children, I have some ideas that could get us out of this rot. I have my outstanding Football Manager career to prove my point.

To Pastor Matthew Keller, thank you for *letting me* steal the way you wrote your acknowledgments. It's brilliant!

AND LAST BUT NOT LEAST

Thanks to God, for dropping this seed in my heart, and helping it grow this big. That Saturday night when I sat in my guest room to put finishing touches on my sermon, I would not have guessed this was your plan all along—and to think I didn't have a convincing end to the sermon! Wow!

God, forgive me for letting this gift lie fallow for as long as I did. I am back. It's time to send the rain of ideas. One ready writer here!

Finally, thanks for revealing all you did during this project. I love the Bible. It makes sense.

I love you, forever!
Victor

about the author

Victor Ehiemere is a thinker, writer and speaker. He is a trained Medical Doctor that has been ruined for ministry, leadership and the pursuit of purpose.

Victor is the Teaching and Creative Arts Pastor at i5 CHURCH, a vibrant community of world-changers in Maryland. Before moving to the USA, Victor was the Senior Pastor of a church that had thousands of young college students pass through its auspices.

Victor is becoming an established voice of sound and clear biblical teaching. He seeks out deep insights and presents then in easily consumable bits. His witty, yet poignant style seeks to push you beyond the edge of mediocrity and nominal living.

Victor, and his beautiful Wife, Dr. Amblessed, live in Maryland with their son, Joel.

Victor has authored two other books, Pursuing Your Purpose and Becoming The Original You. He frequently blogs at www.PastorVictor.com, and can be followed on Social Media @victorehiemere

As a die-hard Arsenal FC fan, he is praying for the return of the league title.

For contact and booking:

Victor Ehiemere
www.pastorvictor.com
@victorehiemere

A portion of the proceeds from the sales of this book goes to i5 ELITE, a registered 501c non-profit organization.

Made in the USA
Middletown, DE
05 June 2016